AN ANTHOLOGY OF MEDIEVAL SERBIAN LITERATURE IN ENGLISH

Mateja Matejić

and

Dragan Milivojević

1978

Slavica Publishers, Inc.
Columbus, Ohio

For a list of some other books from Slavica, see the last pages of this book; for a complete catalog with prices and ordering information, write to:
Slavica Publishers, Inc.
P.O. Box 14388
Columbus, Ohio 43214

ISBN: 0-89357-055-9

Copyright © 1978 by Slavica Publishers, Inc.; all rights reserved.

Text set by Eleanor B. Sapp.

Editor of Slavica Publishers: Charles E. Gribble, The Ohio State University, Columbus.

Printed in the United States of America by LithoCrafters, Inc., Chelsea, Michigan 48118.

TABLE OF CONTENTS

ACKNOWLEDGMENT	7
A NOTE ON CONTRIBUTIONS	7
A LIST OF ABBREVIATIONS	8
TRANSLITERATION AND PRONUNCIATION TABLE	8
MEDIEVAL SERBIAN LITERATURE	9
ON THE LANGUAGE OF MEDIEVAL SERBIAN LITERATURE	22
PRESBYTER FROM DIOCLEA	27
THE KINGDOM OF SLAVS: Legend of Prince Vladislav	28
STEFAN NEMANJA	33
THE HILANDAR CHARTER	33
ST. SAVA [RASTKO NEMANJIĆ]	37
THE LIFE OF SAINT SIMEON:	38
Nemanja's Abdication, His Advice to the the Nobility and His Parting with Them;	38
Nemanja Abdicating, Advises His Sons;	39
Nemanja Sees Death Approaching, Parts with His Son;	41
Nemanja's Last Hours	43
THE OFFICE FOR ST. SIMEON	45
STEFAN NEMANJIĆ [THE FIRST-CROWNED]	47
THE LIFE OF STEFAN NEMANJA:	47
The Birth and Baptism of Nemanja;	
Nemanja is Ruling a Part of His Patrimony;	48
Nemanja's Abdication and His Entrance into the Monastery	49
Praise to St. Simeon	52
DOMENTIJAN	55
THE LIFE OF SAINT SAVA	55
Rastko's Birth;	55
Rastko's Departure for the Holy Mount	58
The Search Party Finds Rastko on the Holy Mount;	60
Rastko Becomes a Monk	61
THE LIFE OF ST. SIMEON	63
Rastko's Departure for the Holy Mount Athos	63
Stefan the First-Crowned's Letter to St. Sava	64
Saint Sava Became an Archbishop and Secured the Serbian Independent Church	65
ATANASIJE	68
Eulogy to St. Sava	68
SILUAN	70

A Hymn to Saint Sava	70
TEODOSIJE	71
THE LIFE OF SAINT SAVA:	71
Saint Sava Having Become an Arhimandrite, Returned to Serbia with Nemanja's Remains	71
THE OFFICE FOR ST. SIMEON	77
THE CANON TO ST. SIMEON	78
THE LIFE OF ST. PETAR OF KORIS	84
TEODOR	89
A Scribe's Inscription	89
NIKODIM OF HILANDAR	92
A Visit to Constantinople	92
JEFIMIJA	94
The Lament Over the Dead Son Overcome by Her Motherly Ways	96
The Encomium to Prince Lazar	96
Prayer to Lord Jesus Christ	98
DANILO II	100
THE LIVES OF SERBIAN KINGS AND ARCHBISHOPS	100
Queen Jelena's Death	100
The Life of St. Milutin	105
The Lament Over Dragutin	108
MILICA HRBELJANOVIĆ [JEVGENIJA]	109
Mother's Prayer	109
Who Is This One?	110
ANONYMOUS MONKS OF RAVANICA	112
The Office for Prince Martyr Lazar	112
Canon to Prince Martyr Lazar	112
Hymn to Prince-Martyr Lazar	119
Milica's Lament	120
DANILO III	122
A Narration about Prince Lazar	122
The Office for St. Malutin	126
STEFAN LAZAREVIĆ	130
The Word of Love	130
The Inscription on the Kosovo Column	132
GRIGORIJE CAMBLAK	134
THE LIFE OF STEFAN DEČANSKI	134
The Youth of Stefan Dečanski	134
Saint Nikolai Appears to the Blinded Stefan	136

  Stefan's Exile to the Monastery of
   Pantokrator in Constantinople and
   His Achievements There   137
  Stefan Dečanski Erects the Dečani
   Monastery As His Legacy   139
  The Story of How Stefan as a Saint
   Defended His Legacy from the Violence
   of a Military Leader   141

A DISCIPLE OF DANILO II   145
 THE LIVES OF SERBIAN KINDS AND ARCHBISHOPS 145
  The Life of Danilo II   145
  The Life of Stefan Dečanski   150

JAKOV OF SER   156
 A Hymn   156

RAJČIN SUDIĆ   158
 An Inscription   158

ISAIJA   159
 Marginal Inscription   159

ISAIJA'S DISCIPLE   162
 LIFE OF ISAIJA   162
  Panegyric to Isaija   162

PRIEST NIKOLA   164
 The Message of a Prisoner   164

PRIEST IVAN   166
 Admission   166

CONSTANTINE THE PHILOSOPHER   167
 THE LIFE OF STEFAN LAZAREVIĆ   167

PRIEST VLKŠA   169
 A Tombstone Inscription   169

DIMITRIJE KANTAKUZIN   170
 A LETTER TO MASTER ISAIJA   171
  Meditation   171
  A Humble Prayer   175

KONSTANTIN MIHAILOVIĆ   184
 NOTES OF A JANISSARY   184

ANONYMOUS   187

The Lament for Djuradj Branković	187
JOVAN OF THE HOLY MOUNT	189
Suffering of a Nation	189
PATRIARCH PAJSIJE	191
THE LIFE OF UROŠ	191
ANONYMOUS	194
Evil Days	194
ANONYMOUS	195
The Song of Death	195
MIHAJLO OF SMEDEREVO	200
Woe, Woe!	200
BIBLIOGRAPHY	201
CONTRIBUTIONS BY MATEJA MATEJIĆ	202
CONTRIBUTIONS BY DRAGAN MILIVOJEVIĆ	203

ACKNOWLEDGMENT

The editors would like to express their sincere gratitude and appreciation to Mr. & Mrs. Mitchell Zunich of Amherst, Ohio for their moral and financial support in the publishing of this book.

The editors also thank Miss Janice Zunich for proofreading the English text.

A NOTE ON CONTRIBUTIONS

The material in this *Anthology of Medieval Serbian Literature* has been written and translated by two editors, Mateja Matejić and Dragan Milivojević; each of them is responsible for the correctness and quality of his own contribution. "The List of Contributions" at the end of the book identifies the contributors and their contributions.

Bibliographical data for each translated text was supplied by its translator. It may be noted that the bibliography is selective and partial rather than complete.

The majority of the works included in this anthology are excerpts; some of the titles of the works have been supplied by the translators.

A LIST OF ABBREVIATIONS

ISSK Bašić, Milivoje. *Iz stare srpske književnosti.* Beograd. 1922.
KFD   Pavlović, Dragoljub & Radmila Marinković. *Iz naše književnosti feudalnog doba.* Sarajevo. 1964.
HMH   Microfilms of Hilandar Slavic Manuscripts at the Main Library of The Ohio State University, Columbus, Ohio.
PK   Novaković, Stojan. *Primeri Književnosti i jezika staroga i srpsko slovenskoga.* Beograd. 1904.
SSK   Pavlović, Dragoljub. *Stara srpska književnost*, 3 volumes. Beograd-Novi Sad: Srpska književna zadruga - Matica Srpska. 1970.
ZIJK *Zbornik za istoriju, jezik i književnost srpskog naroda.* Beograd-Sremski Karlovci. (Volumes and years of publication given separately.)
ŽK   Daničić, Djuro. [Danilo III *Životi kraljeva i arhiepiskopa srpskih.* Zagreb. 1866.
ŽSS   Daničić, Djuro. [Domentijan] *Životi svetog Simeuna i svetog Save.* Beograd. 1865.

TRANSLITERATION AND PRONUNCIATION TABLE

c	pronounced as	ts	in *cats*;
ć	similar, but softer than the *ch*		in *much*;
č	as	ch	in *church*;
dj	as	j	in *Jim*;
dž	as	j	in *John*;
h	as	h	in *host*;
j	as	y	in *yes*;
lj	as	l	in *million*;
nj	as	n	in *foreign*;
s	as	sh	in *bush*;
tz	used instead of *c* only in *tzar*, *tzaritza*, and *tzardom*;		
ž	as	z	in *azure*.

MEDIEVAL SERBIAN LITERATURE

Slavic literacy, introduced in Moravia in 863 A.D. by Constantine (Cyril), his brother Methodius, and their disciples, reached the Serbian lands a decade later, in 873. At that time, Prince Mutimir had consented to the Christianization of his subjects, and the disciples of Cyril and Methodius, who came as missionaries to undertake the task, brought with them codices containing scriptural and liturgical texts. These codices were written in Glagolitic letters. Two or three decades later, the Cyrillic alphabet, introduced around 893 in Simeon's Bulgarian Empire, gradually began to replace the Glagolitic, except on some islands in the Adriatic Sea where it has been preserved to this date.

At the beginning of Serbian literature, the principal literary activity of Serbian scribes consisted of copying the existing Slavic manuscripts whose scriptural and liturgical texts had been translated from Greek by Cyril, Methodius, and their disciples. It is possible, however, that in this period, which lasted from the ninth until the eleventh century, new translations were made among the Serbs.

The selection of the works to be translated from Greek into Slavic was determined by the theological, liturgical, organizational, and educational needs of the Christian Church emerging among the Slavs. The same applied to Serbian medieval literature which was created primarily and exclusively within the Church, for the needs of the Church, and usually by individuals in the service of the Church-- priests and monks. It is, therefore, no wonder that medieval Serbian literature had a predominantly religious content, spirit, tone, and character.

Scriptural and liturgical texts, which represented the "Primers" for the newly-converted Serbs, exerted a two-fold impact on them: religious and esthetic. The Bible, or at least portions of it, abounds in captivating imagery, excellent poetic language, and stylistic perfection. The same is true of liturgical hymns. Thus, the literary taste of the Serbs was developed by their listening to and reading of David's Psalms and the mystical and highly poetic books of the prophets, evangelists, and writers of epistles. Equally important for the development of the

Serbs' literary taste were the liturgical hymns, hagiographies, sermons, and panegyrics written by outstanding Byzantine authors. In a sense, the first Serbian teachers of literature were such excellent writers as John Chrysostomos, Basil the Great, Cyril of Jerusalem, Gregory the Theologian, Gregory of Nyssa, Athanasius of Alexandria, Athanasius of Sinai, Andreas of Crete, Epiphanius of Cyprus, John the Ladderer, Theodoretus, Servianus of Gabala, John Damascene, and many others whose works constituted the first reading material of the Serbs.

In addition to scriptural and liturgical texts, the medieval Serbs had an opportunity to acquaint themselves with historical, canonical, apocryphal, and even secular works from Byzantine literature in Slavic translation.

The active participation of Serbian scribes in copying manuscripts during this period is attested to by the fact that some literary documents preserved from the tenth and eleventh centuries contain orthographic, phonetic, morphological, and lexical features characteristic of the Old Serbian language. These documents were written in Church Slavonic, the common literary language of several medieval Slavic nations. However, the recension was Serbian. Among these documents were *Codex Marianus* and *Glagolita Clozianus*, both from the eleventh century.

During this initial period, Serbian literature was greatly enriched by translations from Greek and original works of Slavic authors from Ochrida and Preslav, the two centers of South Slavic Christendom following the collapse of the Moravian mission in 885. Works of Kliment of Orchrida, Constantine of Preslav, Crnorizac Hrabr, John Exarch, Presbyter Kozma and others were copied and read on the territory of the Serbian state. By the end of the twelfth century, both the volume and the variety of genres of texts translated from Greek, as well as the number of original works of Slavic authors, were considerable.

Coexistent with Old Bulgarian and, later with Old Serbian literature, was the literature of the Bogomils, a medieval socio-religious sect. They did not accept or follow the norms and trends of canonical literature as promoted by the Church. Furthermore, Bogomilism was an anti-feudal and anti-ecclesiastical movement; and the majority of its followers were common people, rather than monks, priests, or nobility. It is, therefore, natural to assume that the literary works of the Bogomils differed significantly from the "canonical" literature, and that many original works may have existed in that now almost completely eradicated literary heritage. Only a few ideas of Bogomilism survived in some "canonical" works where they are to be found primarily in the form of quotations by authors engaged in refuting the teaching of Bogomils.

There are no original works preserved from the earliest period of Serbian literacy and literarure; this does not exclude the possibility that such works existed. The *Tablet of Baška*, an epigraphic monument from the end of the tenth century does indeed contain an original text written in Glagolitic letters. Similar official documents, if not literary works in the narrow sense of the word, may have been written on parchment at princely courts. It is difficult to believe that nothing original was written by the Serbs in the course of three centuries --from the end of the ninth to the end of the twelfth century. It is more probable that original official documents and even literary works were produced, but, as a result of frequent plunderings and devastations inflicted upon Serbian lands by various invaders at various times, such literary material was destroyed. One would hope that some of these documents escaped destruction, and that, eventually, they may be discovered.

The only known eleventh century original literary work as *The Kingdom of Slavs*, written by an anonymous priest from Dioclea (present-day Montenegro). This work, which among other things contained the "Life of St. Vladimir" or "The Legend of Prince Vladimir," has been preserved in the twelfth century work of another anonymous priest from Bar in Dioclea, also entitled *The Kingdom of Slavs*. This work, however, stands apart somehow from the main stream of Serbian medieval literature. There is no evidence that it directly influenced the course of, or initiated a literary tradition in, medieval Serbian literature.

The emergence of original Serbian literature seems to be directly and closely related to the independence of the Serbian Orthodox Church, which, until 1219, was under the jurisdiction of the Archbishopric of Ochrida. Similar to the Russian Orthodox Church, or more correctly, to the Metropolitanate of Kiev, where the introduction of the cult of Boris and Gleb and that of Vladimir were precursors to its ecclesiastical independence, the emergence of the cult of St. Simeon (Stefan Nemanja) directly preceded ecclesiastical independence of the Serbian Orthodox Church granted by Manuelos Sarentinus, the Patriarch of Nicaea in 1219. Sava Nemanjić (hereafter to be referred to as St. Sava), who was instrumental in both the canonization of Simeon and in obtaining ecclesiastical independence, wrote the biography of his father as well as the liturgical hymns for the Office for St. Simeon. Both a biography and liturgical hymns, or an entire Office, are indispensable for the cult of a prospective saint. The biography of his father was not originally written as a separate work, but as a portion of the *Typikon* of Studenica, a monastery in Raška founded by Stefan Nemanja. This typikon was written in 1208, three years after St. Simeon's cult was initiated in the Monastery Hilandar on Mount Athos, Greece, yet before the cult was officially proclaimed by the Church and spread in Raška. In fact, the biography, as well as the hymns necessary for the Office, may well have been conceived shortly after St. Simeon's death in 1200 while St. Sava was still at Hilandar. According to Domentijan's biography of Saint Sava, the latter was commissioned by the elders of Hilandar to write those hymns necessary for the commemoration of Saint Simeon, which were introduced in Hilandar before Saint Simeon's canonization.

St. Sava's biography of St. Simeon is not a full biography but an account of the last three years of St. Simeon's life, and, in particular, an account of his death at Hilandar, witnessed by St. Sava. The outstanding features of this biography are its realistic details and lyricism. These same features can traditionally be found in biographies, or rather, hagiographies, written subsequently by other medieval Serbian hagiographers. Modeled on both Byzantine and early original Slavic hagiographies, medieval Serbian biographies conform to the iconographic method of the protrayal of saints, concentrating on the idealization and creation of their spiritual image rather than on truly biographical data, yet still providing a sufficient amount of factual information regarding their lives.

The literary creativity of St. Sava also includes the writing of church hymns and eulogies incorporated in the Office for St. Simeon. These are the first original poetic forms known in Serbian literature. His "Letter to Spiridon" is a preserved sample of his creativity in the epistolary genre. Finally, his translations and compilations of typika from Greek were a significant contribution to medieval Serbian literature.

The purpose of St. Sava's biography and Office of St. Simeon was evidently related to the establishment of St. Simeon's cult in order to strengthen the position of the Serbian Orthodox Church in its aspiration to ecclesiastical independence. Although this was not the only reason, one should be aware of it.

St. Sava's older brother, Stefan Nemanjić, the First Crowned, ruler of Raška during 1196-1228, also wrote a biography of St. Simeon, but apparently with another purpose in mind. It is a full biography, from birth to death, with an emphasis on Nemanja the Ruler. The purpose of this biography was not only to glorify Simeon the saint, but also Nemanja the ruler, in order to strengthen dynastic rights. Bearing in mind that the biography was completed in 1216, and that in 1217, Stefan was the first Serbian king to receive his crown from the Pope, this conjecture seems justified. Nevertheless, it would not be proper to relate the writing of the biography solely to the question of dynastic legitimacy and obtaining the royal crown. In the biography, St. Simeon is addressed and glorified as a saint, not just a mighty ruler. Indeed, it is impossible to determine what the strongest motivation was for writing this biography, although one may assume that, in addition to Christian and filial motifs, political motivation also entered into the picture.

Stefan's biography of his father is very well written. It is obvious that its author was a well-read person, thoroughly acquainted with biblical texts as well as with the norms of the hagiographic genre. Stefan's artistic mastery is also quite evident.

Domentijan, a very talented medieval Serbian writer, excelled in the genre of hagiographies. His *Life of Saint Simeon*, however, is not entirely original because its largest portion is directly borrowed from Stefan's biography of St. Simeon. Interestingly enough, even his panegyric to St. Simeon contains portions from Hilarion's "Panegyric to St. Vladimir." This illustrates the existence of the mutual influence of medieval Slavic literatures, Mount Athos often being the center of such contact.

Domentijan's best and most important work is his *Life of Saint Sava*, a masterpiece of medieval Serbian literature. It was written in compliance with the literary norms of that genre, primarily for readers at royal courts and in monasteries. Considering the fact that the biography was written in 1253 (though there are literary historians who suggest other dates), the year that the cult of Saint Sava was officially established in Raška, one may assume that this biography was written to aid the establishment of Saint Sava's cult.

Teodosije, a protegé of Domentijan, is actually the most talented and the most prolific medieval Serbian author. His biography of St. Sava, written at the end of the thirteenth century (c.1292) is less "canonical" but more interesting than Domentijan's. It excels in its masterful narration, selectivity of detail, and sense of the dramatic, with a style relatively free of excessive biblical quotations and panegyrical tone.

Teodosije is also credited with the biography of St. Peter of Koriš, a thirteenth century hermit. The author's main idea was to depict Peter as an example of absolute dedication to God, both willing and able to abandon even his closest relatives in order to manifest his love for and obedience to God. In depicting such a hero, positive from the Christian and particularly the monastic point of view, Teodosije actually produced a hero who from the present point of view is negative, deprived of any love for man, insensitive, and almost inhuman.

Teodosije was also a very prolific church hymnographer. He wrote Canons, Offices, individual hymns, and panegyrics to Christ, St. Simeon, St. Sava, and St. Peter of Koriš. Esthetic and literary norms regarding the genre of hymnody in the Orthodox Church were restrictive to a certain extent, interfering with the author's individuality and originality; the hymns had to be written according to the principles and style established in "canonical" church hymns. Teodosije successfully fulfilled the canonical requirements, yet also succeeded in manifesting his originality.

Among the highest achievements in the genre of medieval Serbian biography, one has to include *The Lives of Serbian Kings and Archbishops*, a monumental work written by Danilo II and his anonymous disciples. This work contains the biographies of all the Serbian rulers from the Nemanjić, with the exception of Nemanja, whose biography had already been written by St. Sava, Stefan Nemanjić, and Domentijan; and the biography of Uroš V, which was written later by Patriarch Pajsije. The biography of Jelena, the wife of King Dragutin, was also included in *The Lives of Serbian Kings and Archbishops*. Altogether, there are biographies of five kings, one queen, and ten archbishops, as well as accounts of the installations of three Serbian Patriarchs. This work is equally important as a literary work and a historical document. Its importance and popularity are reflected in the fact that, of all the words of medieval Serbian literature, this was the only one referred to in Serbian folk epic poetry.

The thirteenth and fourteenth centuries are considered to be the Golden Period of medieval Serbian literature. The volume, as well as the quality, of the works produced in this period is very impressive. This is particularly true of biographies, liturgical hymns, eulogies, and panegyrics.

The flourishing of Serbian literature was interrupted by the invasion of Raška by the Turks, followed by five centuries of slavery. However, even after the battle of Kosovo in 1389, which marked the end of the independent Serbian state, Serbian literature continued to flourish for a few more decades. Danilo III, the Serbian Patriarch during 1382-1398, wrote *A Narrative About Prince Lazar* and several hymnographic works. An anonymous writer, most likely a monk, wrote *An Abbreviated Biography of Prince Lazar*, and another, also anonymous, produced *The Life and Reign of Prince Lazar*. Poetic works, which were also produced during this period, will be discussed later.

Prior to 1389, the predominant type of Serbian saint was an ascetic, usually a former ruler or nobleman, who abandoned the pleasures of life, forsook the comfort of his palace, and retreated to a monastery to spend the rest of his life praying, fasting, and practicing monastic virtues. They are praised for having preferred the spiritual over the material, and for having chosen the "heavenly" rather than the "earthly" kingdom. With Lazar, the tragic yet majestic leader of the doomed Serbian army who was slain in the battle with the Turks, a new type of saint appeared. Unlike his predecessors who earned sainthood by asceticism, Lazar earned his sainthood in battle, defending Christianity. He, too, renounced this transitory world, life, and fame, not by retreating to a monastery, but by laying down his life for his "religion and Motherland." His supreme sacrifice and martyr's death became a new theme in Serbian literature; both the Serbian Church and Serbian literature, which until that time had hailed the saint-hermit and the saint-monk, began to praise the saint-martyr--the slain warrior.

The genre of biography continued to be cultivated after the battle of Kosovo and the fall of the Serbian state. Grigorije Camblak, a Bulgarian medieval author left Bulgaria after the fall of Trnovo and the Bulgarian Empire in 1396, settled for a while in Serbia and earned an honorable place in Serbian literature by his *Life of Stefan Dečanski*. A biography of this king had already been written by one of Danilo's disciples and included in *The Lives of Serbian Kings and Archbishops*. However, that biography was written during the reign of Dečanski's son, Stefan Dušan, who is believed to have ordered, or at least consented to, the execution of his father. Danilo's disciple, a subject of Dušan, could not have written an objective biography of Stefan Dečanski. He depicted him as a hateful and vengeful person who had himself to blame for what happened. In fact, there was no mention of his execution, and it was suggested that he died a natural death. His son Dušan was depicted as a patient, obedient, noble son, persecuted by his father for no reason at all. Grigorije Camblak rectified this injustice by his biography of Stefan Dečanski in which he depicted this martyr, blinded by his own father and executed at the request of his son, as an innocent victim.

In a manner similar to his compatriot Grigorije Camblak, another Bulgarian author, Constantine of Kostenica, known as Constantine the Philosopher, a learned man, also left his country after the fall of Trnovo and settled in Serbia. At that time, Stefan Lazarević, Prince Lazar's son, an enlightened ruler and himself an author, founded and supported a cultural center at the Monastery Manasija, referred to as "Resavska Škola" (The School of Resava). Learned men, scribes, writers, and iconographers from Serbia and other territories occupied by the Turks gathered at Manasija, and, for a short period, ending with the death of Stefan Lazarević in 1427, developed a very intensive cultural activity. Painting icons, copying old Serbian and other Slavic manuscripts, translating Greek into Old Serbian, and creating new literary works were some of the activities of this center. Constantine, the head of this center, was also engaged in translating and copying, as well as in writing original works. His "Treatise on Letters" is a very important work, containing rules and regulations for the proposed reform of the Old Serbian language in conformity with reforms introduced in Old Bulgarian by Patriarch Eftimij and his followers in the "School of

Trnovo." He also wrote a biography of his benefactor Stefan Lazarević. At the end of that biography is a very poetic panegyric to Stefan.

Pajsije, the Serbian Patriarch during the period 1614-1648 was the last medieval Serbian hagiographer. At the time that he lived and created, conditions in Serbia, occupied by the Turks, were not favorable for cultural activity and literary creativity. Initially rather tolerant, the Turks soon began to oppress the "raja" (the term used in reference to conquered Christians) without restraint. Pajsije's biography of the mightiest Serbian emperor, Stefan Dušan, was an indirect reminder of the past glory of Serbia, and, thereby, a source of inspiration and strength necessary for preserving Serbian nationalism. His biography of Dušan's son, Uroš V, the last ruler of the Nemanjić dynasty, was an indirect allegation that the present suffering was a consequence of the "sins of our fathers." For the sake of "ideology" in Uroš' biography, Pajsije violated historical fact and deviated from historical truth. Thus, Pajsije accused Vukašin Mrnjavčević, who died in the battle of Marica in 1371, of the murder of Uroš V, who actually died a natural death, also in 1371. Pajsije also wrote a biography of St. Simon (Stefan Nemanjić, the First-Crowned) and an Office for him. Furthermore, he wrote an abbreviated ("prolog") biography of and an Office for Uroš V.

Liturgical poetry, or hymnody, including the traditional types of *stichera*, as well as panegyrics, hymns, and eulogies, was created concurrently with biographies. This specific type of poetry appears in manuscripts in the form of prose, yet its quality and style are poetic. The texts of larger poetic works, *acolutia*, are subdivided into smaller units, *stichera*, corresponding to stanzas. They are written in a flowery, highly metaphorical style, abundant in imagery and rhetorical figures. Some of the eulogies and panegyrics distinguish themselves by the personal feeling and intimate thought of their authors, successfully blended with the abstraction and generalities traditionally present in hymnody. The literary qualities of medieval Serbian hymnody are attested to by the few samples included in this anthology.

As already mentioned, St. Sava was the first known Serbian hymnographer. Later, numerous cults of Serbian saints both created the necessity and provided the opportunity for authors to produce more works in the hymnody genre. Teodosije, one of the most prolific hymnographers, wrote Canons and complete Offices for St. Simeon, St. Sava, and St. Peter of Koriš. Atanasije, Teodosije's contemporary, was credited by Domentijan with the authorship of a "Hymn to St. Sava," which, according to Domentijan, Atanasije delivered orally on the occasion that the remnants of St. Sava were brought from Trnovo to the Monastery Mileševa. Siluan, a monk of Mount Athos and another contemporary of Teodosije, Jakov of Ser, a Serbian hierarch in the fourteenth century and the Disciple of Isaija, also from the fourteenth century, each left only a short hymn, yet the literary quality of their hymns justifies their being included in the history of medieval Serbian literature. Poetic passages also exist in Danilo's *The Lives of Serbian Kings and Archbishops*. An example is "The Lament Over Dragutin," included in this anthology.

A more productive and more important hymnographer is Danilo III. His *Office for St. Milutin* is a good illustration of his poetic talent. Some of his contemporaries, monks of the Monastery Ravanica, also left a precious contribution to Serbian medieval hymnody, but, regretfully, did not disclose their identity. *The Office for Prince Lazar*, "Hymn to Prince Martyr Lazar," and "Lament Over Djuradij Branković" are but a few samples of the poetic works produced by this anonymous authors.

The two women authors included in this anthology, Milica Hrebeljanović and Jelena Mrnjavčević, or Jevgenija and Jefimija, as they were known by their monastic names, made outstanding contributions to medieval Serbian literature. Their works, poetic and elegiac, added a feminine touch to the predominantly monastic and masculine literature, and left a testimony to the fact that education and literary talent were not a property exclusive to medieval Serbian men. Both of these women lived in the same historical period; in fact, they lived together at the court of Prince Lazar--Milica as his wife, and Jelena as a refugee. Both had a tragic life, and both expressed their grief through poetry.

Jefimija's authorship of "The Lament for the Lost Child," "Prayer Embroided on the Curtain of Hilandar," and "Encomium to Prince Lazar" is uncontested, although the largest portion of her inscription on the curtain of Hilandar is borrowed from the prayers of John Chrysostomos, Simeon Metaphrast, and Simeon the New Theologian.

Jevgenija's authorship of "A Mother's Prayer" can hardly be contested, for it is a portion of an edict to the

Monastery Dečani, issued by Jevgenija and her two sons, Stefan and Vuk. However, her authorship of "Who Is This One?"(the title has been supplied by the translator) is questioned.

The authorship of the *Office for Prince Martyr Lazar* and the *Office Commemorating the Transfer of Prince Martyr Lazar's Relics* is also an unsettled question. Anonymous monks of the Monastery Ravanica, Grigorije Camblak, Danilo III, and Jefimija are considered by various literary historians as the probable authors of portions of these two Offices. All of them agree that these Offices are not the works of a single author, and the majority of them agree that Danilo III is the author of "A Narration About Prince Martyr Lazar" which is included in the *Office Commemorating the Transfer of Prince Martyr Lazar's Relics*.

Lazar and Milica's (Jevgenija) son, Stefan Lazarević, was also an outstanding medieval Serbian author. Even if he did not write all the works attributed to him, his writing of "The Word of Love" alone would fully justify his being included in the history of medieval Serbian literature, because of the artistic excellence of that work. However, his authorship of both "The Word of Love" and "The Inscription on the Kosovo Column" is disputed. For instance, Djordje Sp. Radojičić, an eminent Serbian literary historian, is inclined to believe that "The Word of Love" is the work of Stefan's mother Jevgenija, whereas some other literary historians simply treat this work as the creation of some unknown author. In this anthology, Stefan is credited with the authorship of "The Word of Love" because the arguments speaking in favor of it are more convincing than those disputing it. "The Inscription on Kosovo Column" is also attributed to him, although it is almost impossible to provide convincing evidence proving this.

Constantine the Philosopher (of Kostenica) and, particularly, Grigorije Camblak, also distinguished themselves as hymnographers. A lament for Stefan Lazarević, included in his biography by Constantine, is quite obviously a poetic work. As for Grigorije, he wrote a complete *Office for St. Stefan Dečanski* as well as *The Office for St. Petka (Paraskeva)*. Other literary works of Grigorije, related to Bulgarian saints, are not mentioned here.

Dimitrije Kantakuzin, an accomplished hymnographer from the fifteenth century, wrote several works of exquisite beauty. His poetic works are his hymns to St. John of Rila, "Prayer to Theotokos," and "Encomium to St. Demetrios." No less poetic, although written in prose, is his "Letter to Master Isaija," excerpts of which are included in this anthology under the title "Meditations." The mood of that work, a pronounced concern with death, almost to the point of obsession, is also present in the "Poem of Death" by an anonymous author.

Patriarch Pajsije, who ends the long line of medieval Serbian biographers, concludes the list of eminent Serbian hymnographers. His two Offices, for St. Simon (Stefan Nemanjić, the First-Crowned) and Uroš V, were not the last Offices in Serbian literature, but they appeared at the end of the period of medieval Serbian literature and were produced within the territory of the medieval Serbian kingdom. After 1690, when some 10,000 Serbian families migrated to Austro-Hungary, the new cultural and literary center emerged in that territory. There the tradition of writing hymnody was continued, although it was also the start of a new period in Serbian literature.

The work of Konstantin Mihailović from Orahovica is an eyewitness' account of the historical events taking place at the end of the Byzantine Empire, including some events related to Serbian history. It is a personal, subjective view of a participant in the tragic events leading to the end of the Serbian and Byzantine Empires. In addition, it is an account of a Christian who, as a Turkish prisoner, had to fight against Christians.

Information concerning historical and social conditions of medieval Serbia is also contained in marginal inscriptions, introductions, and afterwords included in liturgical and scriptural codices. The tragedy of the country and the suffering of the people are two recurrent themes in these medieval notes, as may be seen from the inscriptions of Rajčin Sudić, Isaija, Mihajlo "the Sinner," and Jovan of the Holy Mount. In other cases, inscriptions contain purely historical references (Nikodim and Vlkša), a personal meditation on the transitoriness of this world (Mihajlo of Smederevo), and even humorous remarks, quite unexpected in the margins of "holy books" (Ivan).

In the course of nine centuries of Serbian literacy, from the ninth through the seventeenth century and in the six centuries of original medieval Serbian literature, from the twelfth through the seventeenth century, medieval Serbian writers produced a valuable literary legacy.

Some of it has been translated into contemporary Serbo-Croatian and is known to Serbian readers. Yet, the largest portion of this literature, written in Church Slavonic, has not even been translated into Serbo-Croatian, let alone foreign languages, and is known only to a handful of specialists interested in Old Serbian literature who are capable of reading it in Church Slavonic.

The editors of this anthology, in which excerpts from medieval Serbian literature appear for the first time in English translation, believe that it will enable the English speaking reader who has not mastered either Church Slavonic or Serbo-Croatian to become acquainted with this cultural heritage of medieval Serbia, which is, at the same time, a legacy for all humanity. They also hope that this book will be of some use to teachers and students of medieval Slavic literatures. Finally, they hope that thousands of Americans and other English speaking individuals of Serbian descent will find this book useful in acquainting themselves with the literary heritage of their forefathers.

ON THE LANGUAGE OF MEDIEVAL SERBIAN LITERATURE

The territory that is known as Yugoslavia today was divided into two cultural zones in the 10th century: the Western Zone, where the Glagolitic alphabet was used based on the ČA dialect, and the Eastern Zone, where the Cyrillic alphabet was used based on the ŠTO dialect. This division, often called the Croatian and Serbian variants of Old Church Slavic, was not rigid in any of the three points mentioned: alphabet, dialect, or nationality. Many Croatian ČA and ŠTO[1] speakers used the Cyrillic alphabet until the Latin alphabet supplanted both the Glagolitic and the Cyrillic alphabet.

As far as medieval Serbian literature is concerned, the use of Cyrillic alphabet based on the Štokavian dialect of the "E" and "jE"[2] subdivisions was carried on consistently from the 12th century until the first decades of the 19th century. Literary activity in all its various forms: charters to monasteries, lives of the saints, apocryphal literature, translated literature, private letters, etc., was centered in the medieval nucleus of the Serbian state, the upper reaches of the mountainous rivers of Tara, Piva, and Lim.

According to Constantine Porphyrogenetos, it included the province of Raška, Dioclea (Montenegro), Zahumlje and Hum (Hercegovina), and Bosnia. The acceptance of the Cyrillic alphabet in these regions was matched by another milestone in Serbian cultural history: the use of Old Church Slavic as the language of literature originally written by the clergy for religious purposes. Old Church Slavic was nothing but a Slavic dialect used near Thessalonica (northern Greece), a South Slavic dialect of the Eastern group very similar in lexis and grammar to the Western South Slavic subdialects used by the Serbs.[3] Old Church Slavic became the literary language, the prestigious language of the Church, emanating from Serbian medieval ecclesiastic centers; as such, it exerted a powerful influence on the history of Serbian literature and the Serbo-Croatian language. From the first Old Serbian manuscript, the Gospel of Miroslav in 1197, until the reforms of Vuk Karadžić in the beginning of the 19th century, literary activity existed in a mixture of two linguistic mediums: Old Serbian and Old Church Slavic.[4] The usage of these two mediums differ according to the choice of the literary "genre," while the intrinsic differences are based on their lexis, phonemic inventory, declensional and conjugational paradigms.

The choice of the literary form, to a great extent, determined the predilection for the predominance of one or the other linguistic component. Lives of Serbian rulers (žitija) were written in the high, hagiographic, Old Church Slavic literary style, imitating and repeating the motive, topoi, metaphors, and set expressions of similar Byzantine works.

On the other hand, private correspondence of Serbian rulers, with Dubrovnik apart from the introductory Old Church Slavic formulas, were written in Old Serbian. When the need for clarity and understanding became imperative, one resorted to Old Serbian.

There are considerable linguistic and stylistic differences within a single literary form. Apart from the Byzantine literary heritage embodied in Old Church Slavic, there is also the influence of oral folk tradition in Old Serbian. The former exists in the presentations and descriptions of war activities, diplomatic negotiations, and ceremonies in the lives of the Serbian rulers. The latter is in topical situations where the folk tradition has already provided the framework: laments, curses, as well as personal emotional situations whose informality dictated the use of an informal linguistic medium. The death lament for Stefan Uroš II and Milutin by Danilo II stand out from the rest of the text by their rhythmic structure, as well as by their language, which differs only slightly from contemporary Serbo-Croatian.

> O oxь mne, sladьkyi moi gospodi po čьto vь skore razluči se otь nasь pastyru dobryi i xranitelju naš blažu mnogopresvetloje lice tvoje ozarьšeje se otь presvetaago duxa imьže i mnogorazumьnyi svetь vьsija namь i imenemь sily kreposti tvojeje lьstь i šatanija i sily lukavyje bezbožьnyix poganь razoriše se .....etc.[5]

The deathbed legacy of Nemanja to his son Sava is permeated by a personal and emotional tone avoiding cumbersome Old Church Slavic expressions and using the simple address of Old Serbian.

> Syne, moju premudrostь vьnimai kь moimь že slovesemь prilagai svoje uxo, da sьxranivši moju myslь blagu, čjuvьstvije že mojeju ustьnu povedaju tebe. Xrani, syne, zakonь otьca tvojego, ne otvrьzi nakazanija mater tvoje ....etc.[6]

Important for the history of the Serbo-Croatian language are occurrences which have influenced the language indirectly and made the history of the Serbo-Croatian language resemble a series of sudden transitions instead of a normal, uninterrupted development. The Turkish conquest in the 14th and the 15th century caused widespread dislocation and migration of the population in a northwestern direction. It is no wonder that the 14th and 15th centuries were often mentioned as a dividing line between the two epochs in the history of the Serbo-Croatian. The main outline of the nominal paradigms has been already completed; the Turkish conquest completely changed the dialect map of Yugoslavia, forcing the ŠTO speakers to move out into the territory of the ČA speakers, thereby restricting their territory.

One would also expect that the interrelationship of Old Church Slavic and Old Serbian in the Old Serbian recension would result in the gradual and progressive predominance of Old Serbian to the detriment of Old Church Slavic. This, actually, did not occur. This was due to the conservatism of the clergy which adhered to the old norms of orthography and Old Church Slavic grammar. The orthographic reform of Constantine the Philosopher, in the 15th century, was a step in that direction. Its purpose was to strengthen and maintain the faith by realizing the orthographic uniformity based on old, authentic manuscripts. The manuscripts of the Resava School, although orthographically uniform, did not reproduce the original Old Church Slavic of Bible translations. Many of the innovations increased the complexity of the orthography, and the syntax and style became turgid and involved. The prestige, however, of the Resava School went beyond the Serbian state of Despot Stevan Lazarević. Copies of the manuscripts of the Resava School were made in Macedonia and in Bulgaria. In Serbia, Resava orthography in the 18th century was simplified. The orthographic conventions reinstated in the reform of Constantine the Philosopher, were now completely and definitely eliminated. A final point in the development of the Serbian recension had been reached when all Old Church Slavic symbols were eliminated and replaced by symbols for Serbian sounds.

In the beginning of the 18th century (1730), Serbian literature in the so-called Serbo-Slavic language (srpskoslovenski) experienced a major outside influence which resulted in the replacement of Serbo-Slavic linguistic norms by the Russian-Slavic (ruskoslovenski).[7] This event can be compared to the adoption of the Old Church Slavic language as the literary language in the 9th and 10th centuries. In both cases, for different reasons, the Serbs accepted a foreign language as their literary language. The immediate reason for the arrival of Russian teachers and Russian books in the Russian recension of Old Church Slavic was the desire of the Serbian clergy in Austria-Hungary to ally itself to the Orthodox Russian clergy and, thereby, to resist the pressure of the privileged Catholic Church in Austria-Hungary. The authority of the Serbian Orthodox Church spread the new linguistic innovations, and from religious literature they were introduced into the secular. Thus, a new complex situation arose in the Serbian literary language of the time, enabling an uneasy synthesis of two literary and linguistic norms to evolve: the Serbian recension of Old Church Slavic with the Russian recension of Old Church Slavic. Added to this were two outside factors: the increase in the influence of the spoken Serbian language through the Serbian recension and the added adherence to the Russian recension. The absence of set linguistic and grammatical norms allowed each writer his choice of lexical material and grammatical forms from the two or three sources mentioned above.

The final solution of this increasingly chaotic and unsettled situation in Serbian literature took place in the early 19th century. The orthographic and linguistic reforms of Vuk Karadžić were one of the most significant turning points in the history of Serbian literature. They could be compared, in their radical departure, with the acceptance of the Cyrillic script and Old Church Slavic as the literary language of the 10th and the 11th centuries. The introduction of spoken Serbian of the štokavian jekavski dialect as the literary Serbian language represented another radical break with the 7th-century old tradition of an Old Church Slavic and the Serbian recension of Old Church Slavic in its different varieties.[8]

NOTES

[1] ČA, ŠTO, and KAJ mean 'what' in Serbo-Croatian and represent the three main dialects.
[2] The reflexes of the common Slavic Ě.

³There are indications in Greek sources that the first habitat of the Serbs after their immigration to the Balkan Peninsula was the area around Thessalonica (Northern Greece) called Serbia and that the Serbs left that area to move to the Southwestern part of Yugoslavia.

⁴Known as the Serbian recension of Old Church Slavic.

⁵Djura Daničić, *Životi kraljeva i arhiepiskopa srpski*, 1866, p. 157.

⁶Stojan Novaković, *Primeri književnosti i jezika staroga i srpskoslovenskoga*, Beograd, 1889, p. 183.

⁷The Russian recension of Old Church Slavic.

⁸Few Slavic words of the Serbian recension of Old Church Slavic and the Russian recension of Old Church Slavic remained in the newly created Serbian literary language, e.g., *opšti, sveštenik*, those with the prefix VA, *vasiona* for the former and *dveri, čest* for the latter.

PRESBYTER FROM DIOCLEA[1]
12TH CENTURY

A few biographical notes identifying this author have been preserved in the introductory portion of his pseudo-historical work, *The Kingdom of Slavs*. This 12th century literary work, preserved in its Latin version only, may have been originally written in Slavic, or, at least, that a portion of the material included in it definitely existed previously in the Slavic language. This is evident from the following remark by the author: "Requested by you, my beloved brethren in Christ and honorable priests of the holy Archbishopric See of the Church in Dioclea, as well as by some elders, but especially by the youth of our city who find pleasure not only in listening to and reading about the wars, but in taking part in them also, to translate from the Slavic language into Latin the work entitled in Latin *Regnum Sclavorum* in which all their deeds and wars have been described..."

It has been generally agreed that the Presbyter from Bar in Dioclea included in his work from folklore and literary material from Slavic sources which he translated into Latin. Among the material he translated, rather than created, is "The Legend of Prince Vladimir" which is supposed to have been written by another clergyman from Dioclea, more specifically, from Krajina in Dioclea. In its original version, it was a hagiographic work, a "Life of St. Vladimir" rather than a "Legend." Prince Vladimir, the protagonist of the story, as well as King Vladislav, who ordered Vladimir's execution, were historical persons, yet "The Legend of Prince Vladimir" contains a number of non-historical details. Another interesting fact concerning this work is that, although actually a hagiography, it contains some "novelistic" material which provides interesting reading even for the sophisticated reader of the 20th century.

Finally, one should mention that notwithstanding the fact that the kingdom of which the Presbyter from Bar narrates in his *The Kingdom of Slavs* is legendary rather than historical, Mavro Orbini, the well-known author of *Il Regno dei Slavi* which was written in Italian and published in 1601, borrowed the title of the Presbyter's *The Kingdom of Slavs* and based his account on the information contained in that book.

NOTES

[1]*Duklja* in the Serbo-Croatian language, formerly an independent kingdom on the territory of present day Montenegro.

THE KINGDOM OF SLAVS
"Legend of Prince Vladimir"

Vladimir[1] was kept in prison, where he was fasting and praying day and night. [Once] the angel of God appeared to him in a vision, encouraging him and announcing to him that God would free him from that prison; and, that through martyrdom, he would reach the Kingdom of Heaven and receive an unwithering wreath and the reward of everlasting life. Then the blessed one, strengthened by the angelic vision, engaged in praying and fasting even more. However, one day, the daughter of the emperor Samuilo,[2] named Kosara, moved and inspired by the Holy Spirit, came to her father and asked his permission to go to the prison, together with her maids, and wash the heads and feet of the chained prisoners and captives; and her father granted her wish. And thus she went and accomplished a good deed. On that occasion, she noticed Vladimir; and, having realized that he was handsome in appearance, modest, gentle, and humble, and that he was full of knowledge and divine wisdom, she spent considerable time conversing with him. His speech seemed to her sweeter than honey and honeycomb. And she became fond of him, not out of passion, but moved by pity for his youth and beauty; and because she had heard that he was a king born in a royal family. [Then] after having said goodbye to him, she left. After that, wishing to free him from captivity, she went to the emperor; and, having prostrated herself before his feet, she spoke thus: "My father and lord, I know that you will find me a husband, as it is customary. Now, therefore, if it pleases your lordship, either give me for a husband King Vladimir, whom you keep in fetters, or be informed that I would rather die than take another man for a husband." After the emperor had heard this, he was glad; and being very fond of his daughter and knowing that Vladimir was of royal family by birth, he gladly consented to grant her wish. And he sent immediately [his servants] after

Vladimir and commanded that, bathed and clad in royal attire, the latter be brought before him. And, looking at him with kindness and kissing him in front of all the noblemen of his state, he gave to him in marriage his own daughter. And then, after the wedding of his daughter was celebrated in accordance with royal customs, the emperor installed Vladimir as a king and gave him the land and kingdom of his ancestors and the entire country of Drač. After that, the emperor sent the message to Dragomir, King Vladimir's uncle, to come and take the land of Trivunia [which had belonged to him], to gather his people, and settle them [there]; and this indeed happened.

Thus, King Vladimir lived with his wife Kosara in piety and chastity, honoring God and serving Him day and night. And he ruled the people entrusted to him righteously and in the fear of God.

After a short time, Emperor Samuilo died and his son Radomir inherited the empire. He was strong and brave and he conducted many wars against the Greeks during the reign of Emperor Basil[3] from whom he captured the entire territory as far as Constantinople. And Emperor Basil, fearing lest he should lose his empire, secretly sent envoys to Vladislav, Radomir's cousin, with the following message: "Why don't you avenge the blood of your father?[4] Take as much gold and silver from me as you want, be at peace with us, and you shall get the kingdom of Samuilo who murdered your father and your brother. If possible, kill his son Radomir who now rules the kingdom." When Vladislav heard this he agreed and one day when Radomir was hunting and he [Vladislav] was riding next to him, he struck him and killed him. And thus Radomir died, and Vladislav, who killed him, reigned in his place.

After he had taken the empire in this manner, he sent his envoys to King Vladimir [inviting him] to come to him. When Kosara the Queen heard this, she asked him not to go, saying, "My lord, do not go lest—God forbid!—what happened to my brother happens to you, too; but allow me to go and see and hear how things are with the king. If he wants to execute me, let him kill me, only you must not die." And thus the queen [with] the king's permission went to her cousin's and she was received with great honors, but deceitfully.

Then, he [Vladislav] sent his envoys to the king once more and sent him as a present a golden cross and a sworn promise, saying, "Why do you hesitate to come? Look, your wife is here with me and no evil has happened to her, but I and my own treat ner decently. Accept the promise [of which] this cross [is the warranty] and come and let me see you; and then you shall return to your domicile with honor and gifts, together with your wife." The king sent him this reply: "We know that our Lord Jesus Christ, who suffered for us, was not crucified on a golden or silver cross, but on the wooden one; if, therefore, your promise and your words are sincere, let some of the clergy bring me a wooden cross, and then, trusting your promise and the power of our Lord Jesus Christ and having faith in the life-creating cross and the precious wood, I shall come."

Then he [Vladislav] summoned two bishops and a monk-hermit, and, concealing from them his treachery, he gave them a wooden cross and dispatched them to the king. They came and greeted the king and conveyed to him the promise and the cross. And the king, having received the cross, made a low bow [before it], kissed it, put it on his chest, and then, with a small retinue, went to the emperor.

In the meantime, the emperor had issued the order for ambushes to be set along the road so that when he [Vladimir] would go by, they would attack him from behind and kill him. But the Almighty God, who protected His servant from his very childhood, did not want to ignore the deeds of men, and He sent His angels to protect him. And as he was passing by the places where the ambushes were set, those who were in ambush noticed that the king was accompanied by soldiers who appeared to have wings and carried signs of victory in their hands; and realizing that they were the angels of God, they [the soldiers] became frightened and fled each to his own area. And the king arrived at the emperor's palace in the city called Prespa; and, as soon as he had entered it, he started praying to God, as was his custom.

When the emperor learned of the king's arrival, he was very angry. He had hoped secretly that the king would be killed on the road before coming to him so that it would not be known that he was an accomplice in the murder or that he consented to it, for he had given a sworn promise, and he had given the cross to the bishops and the monk hermit; that was why he had set the ambush along the road. But when he realized that his dirty work had been discovered, he sent the executioners to kill him [Vladimir] while he [the emperor] was having lunch.

While the king was praying, the soldiers surrounded him. When the king noticed it, he sent for the bishops and the monk-hermit who were there and said, "What is this, my gentlemen? What did you do? Why did you deceive me in such a manner? Why should I die innocent because I trusted your words and the sworn promises?" And they were so ashamed that they could not look him in the eyes. Then the king offered prayers to God, made his confession, and received the Body and Blood of the Lord; and holding the cross which he had received from the emperor in his hand, he said, "Pray for me, my gentlemen, and may this precious cross together with you testify on the Lord's Day [Last Judgment] that I am dying innocent." Then he kissed the cross, made peace with the bishops and took leave from them; and while everybody was crying, he left the church and the soldiers killed him right in front of the door of the church: he was decapitated on May 22. And the bishops took his body and buried it in that same church, [chanting funeral-] hymns and [offering] eulogies.

And the Lord, in order to manifest the merits of the blessed martyr Vladimir, effected the healing of many people afflicted by various illnesses as soon as they entered the church and prayed at his tomb. At night, however, they all saw a divine light, as if many candles were lit.

And the wife of the blessed Vladimir wept bitterly in the course of many days, [so bitterly] that it is impossible to describe.

When the emperor saw the miracles which God performed there, he repented, became very afraid, and allowed his cousin to take [Vladimir's] relics and bury them where she wanted. Eventually, she took the relics and transfered them to the place known as Krajina, where his [Vladimir's] palace used to be, and buried them in the church of St. Mary. His relics still lay there and issue a pleasant fragrance as if anointed with many aromatic substances. And the cross which he had [once] received from the emperor is still in his hands.

NOTES

[1] A historical person, the ruler of Dioclea, murdered by Vladislav c. 1016.
[2] 976-1014, the founder of Macedonian Empire.
[3] Byzantine Emperor Basil the Second, 976-1025.

[4]Vladislav's father, Aron, was executed at the order of Samuilo.

Sources:

Latin text and Serbo-Croatian translation published in
    Šišić, Ferdo. *Letopis popa Dukljanina*. Posebno
    izdanje Srpske akademije nauka. Beograd, 1928.
Serbo-Croatian text only published in: *KFD*; *SSK*;
    Novaković, Stojan. *Prvi osnovi slovenske
    književnosti*. Beograd, 1893.

STEFAN NEMANJA
c. 1132-1200

Stefan Nemanja was the indisputable founder of both the independent Serbian state and the Nemanjić dynasty. As ruler of Raška (Serbia) in the period of 1168-1196, he made Orthodoxy the official religion in his state, strengthened the Orthodox Church, and founded and financed many churches and monasteries. In 1196, he renounced the throne in favor of his son Stefan and went to Mount Athos, where he became a monk and took the name Simeon. Together with his son Sava, who was a monk at Mount Athos, Simeon built the Hilandar Monastery in 1198-1199. This beautiful monastery, which is still in existence, has been a cultural and religious center of the Serbian Orthodox Church for centuries. The necessary charter for the newly-founded monastery was issued by Simeon, although it is alleged to have been written by St. Sava. The introductory part of the charter contains some autobiographical details which were presumably dictated by Simeon himself. In addition, that portion of the charter presents views on the source of imperial, royal, and princely authority, and these views are ascribed to Simeon. He died in 1200 at Hilandar and was buried there. Later, St. Sava transferred his remains to Raška. At that time, Simeon was canonized. St. Sava used the authority of his saintly father to end the civil war which was raging in Raška and to reconcile his two warring brothers: Vukan, who was bypassed by his father as the heir to the throne, and Stefan, who was younger than Vukan, but who was chosen by his father to rule Raška.

THE HILANDAR CHARTER

"In the beginning God created the heaven and the earth"[1] and the people on it, blessing them and giving them power over all his creation; he appointed emperors to some, to others princes and rulers, and he allowed everyone to graze his own flock and guard it from all evil which might fall upon it. Therefore, oh brothers, the most merciful God appointed emperors for the Greeks, kings for the Hungarians, and separating the peoples, he gave each one laws and customs, establishing rulers over them and separating them according to the customs and laws in his wisdom. Because of his great and unlimited mercy and his love of humanity, he presented our great-grandfathers and our grandfathers with the rule of these Serbian lands, and working for the betterment of the people and not wishing them to perish, he appointed me the great Župan,[2] called in holy baptism Stefan Nemanja. I have restored my ancestral land and strengthened it even more with the wisdom and assistance given to me by God. I raised my crumbling ancestral land and acquired from the coastal regions Zeta[3] with its towns; from the Albanians, Pilot;[4] and from the Greek land, Lab[5] with Lipljani,[6] Globočica,[7] Reke Zarlata,[8] Levča,[9] Belica[10] and Lepenica.[11] Having acquired all this with God's help and my labor, and having secured with God's aid peace and the endorsement of my rule from all sides, I began to meditate and educate my mind to take care and be anxious about my soul so as to know on what date I would undergo the day of holy judgment and be able to accept the angelic and apostolic image and Christ's words: "Take my yoke upon you and learn of me; for I am meek and lowly in heart; and ye shall find rest unto your souls. For my yoke is easy and my burden is light."[12] After much time passed away, my most merciful Lord did not scorn the prayer of his own creation, but as a generous defender and dispenser of rewards said with his pure mouth, "I came not to call the righteous, but sinners to repentence."[13] And because of his mercy, everything occurred to me at that time suddenly and clearly. All the honor and glory of this whole world I began to consider as worthless; and all the beauty of this life, with its attractive forms and shapes, now appeared to me as smoke; and only Christ's love attached evermore to me, although I was unworthy of it. I left my throne and my family and my different possession immediately as Christ and the holy lady Mother of God wanted it; and I, the sinner, was aligned with his gentle burden; and he ordained me a member in the monastic rank, the small one as well as the great one. After this happened to me and I arranged all this, I left on my throne, in charge of the dominion bestowed upon me by Christ, my beloved son Stefan, great Župan and Sevastokrator,[14] the son-in-law of King Aleksij,[15] the Greek Emperor who was crowned by God. I, by the name of Simeon, the monk, although an unworthy servant of Christ, blessed him with all kinds of blessings, as Isaac blessed his son Jacob. Let the Lord help him in every good deed in his dominion, and let him be friendly to the Christian world; let him take care of the churches and of those who serve in them, and let the creator and the Lord in no way be reproached. Afterwards, by the wish of my Lord Christ, as the writing says: "No prophet is accepted in his own country,"[16] the thought occurred to me to leave my friends and children and to move to some place where I could receive my salvation. My Lord did not abandon me and deprive me of my wish; he even rejoiced in the sinner who was repenting. I left my fatherland for Mount Athos and found a monastery which once had been called Hilandar,[17] dedicated to the holy presentation of our Most Glorious Lady, the Mother of God. It was all in ruins, demolished from all sides. So I worked in my old age, and with the help of my son, the great Župan Stefan, the Lord deigned me to be its restorer. I searched for its broken-down remnants and restored them; and, according to the wish of our lady, the Mother of God, I requested and obtained from the emporer in Prizren many tenant farmers. I gave some of them to the monastery on Mount Athos of the holy Mother of God in Mileji,[18] as well as some to the villages of Neprobišta,[19] Momuša,[20] Slamodrava,[21] Retivla,[22] Trnye,[23] Retivštica,[24] Trnovac,[25] Hoča,[26] and another Hoča,[27] along with the income from the marketplace and two vineyards which I planted in the area.

I set up four beehives: the first in Trpezi,[28] the second in Dabšor,[29] the third in Gološevo[30] and the fourth in Parice,[31] with two men attending each beehive. To the monastery, I also donated Mount Bogača[32] and the cattle villages of Rodovo,[33] Sudstvo,[34] and Djurdjivo,[35] along with 170 cattlemen and as much cattle as I could. I donated horses and 30 bushels of salt from Zeta. If anyone attached to the monastery were to flee to the great Župan or to someone else, he should be brought back; and if someone under the Župan's jurisdiction were to join the monastery men, he would be brought back again. Everything I have donated to the monastery on Mount Athos should be coveted neither by my children, nor by my grandchildren and relatives, nor by anyone else. Whoever alters this, let God judge him; and let his antagonist on that last judgment be the holy Mother of God and I, Simeon the sinner.

Simeon's Cross

and Signature

NOTES

[1] Genesis 1:1. The biblical quotations were, for the most part, freely translated, as they did not follow consistently the biblical passages. St. Stanojević, D-r.; D. Glumac, *Sv. Pismo U Našim Starim Spomenicima*, Beograd, 1932, Posebna Izdanja, Book 39, Srpska Kraljevska Akademija, provided guidance in this matter. There are two types of biblical quotations in the text: 1) quotations from memory which did not follow the Bible exactly, and 2) quotations which followed the Biblical text closely. The latter were incorporated from the Bible. It should be taken into account that even in those cases the quotations do not follow the biblical passages sequentially without any omissions. The Authorized King James Version was followed throughout the translation.

[2] The ruler of several clans.

[3] The area north of Lake Scutari in the present Republic of Montenegro in Southwest Yugoslavia. This area had been also known as Zeta.

[4] A village near Prizren and the adjoining area.

[5] The river Lab near the river Sitnica in the Kosovo area.

[6] A village near Priština and the adjoining area.

[7-11] Stefan Prvovenčani refers to all these regions as Oblast Nisavask.

[12] Matthew 11:29-30.

[13] Mark 2:17

[14] Ruler.

[15] Alexius IV Angelus

[16] Luke 4:24

[17] The restoration of the Hilandar monastery started in 1198 when this monastery was given to Stefan Nemanja and Saint Sava by the Byzantine Emperor Alexius IV. This monastery remained the center of the spiritual culture of the Serbs during the reign of the Nemanjić dynasty.

[18] A monastery on Mount Athos.

[19-35] Villages near Prizren in the south of Yugoslavia.

Sources

The original manuscript is located in the Monastery of
   Hilandar on Mount Athos. Šafarik published it in
   Pamatky Drevniho Pisemnictvy Jihoslovanuv in Prague
   in 1851.

ST. SAVA [RASTKO NEMANJIĆ]
(1175-1235)

Rastko Nemanjić, the youngest son of Stefan Nemanja and his wife Anna, left the court of his father in his early youth and went to the Holy Mount (Mt. Athos in Greece) where he became a monk and took the name Sava. He is certainly the most outstanding person in all of Serbian history. He was the founder, organizer, and leader of the national Serbian Orthodox Church, and, in addition, was an enlightener of his people, an able statesman, a successful peacemaker, a talented writer, and, in fact, the organizer of monastic life in Raška. St. Sava was also the founder of Serbian literature.

In addition to some purely ecclesiastic canonical works, which were translations and adaptations from Greek rather than original works, St. Sava wrote a biography of his father Stefan Nemanja, *Office for St. Simeon*, and some letters and charters.

St. Sava's biography of his father marks the beginning of original Serbian literature. Similar to hagiography, a genre inherited from Byzantine literature, this biography, as well as the biographies written later by other Serbian medieval authors, differs from hagiography in many aspects. The number of realistic details and lyrical elements is much higher than in traditional hagiographies. First person narration, used in Serbian medieval biographies, is also unusual for hagiographies. Furthermore, in writing the biography of his father, St. Sava made no attempt to conceal his filial sentiments.

Although the purpose of the biography of Stefan, or rather Simeon Nemanja, his monastic name, was to praise not the ruler but the monk, thereby indirectly glorifying monasticism; it is, nevertheless, a touching account of the last few years of St. Simeon, as observed by his son. St. Sava, the son who, contrary to the wishes of his parents and without their permission, abandoned the mundane glory in favour of monastic life, paid tribute to his father, who had also abandoned the power and glory of his princely court and exchanged it for saintly monastic life.

The Life of Saint Simeon

Nemanja's Abdication, His Advice to the Nobility and His Parting with Them

After Nemanja had completed thirty-seven years[1] of rule, the most merciful Lord did not neglect his prayers, which came with a sigh from the depth of his heart; and being generous, industrious, and the dispenser of rewards to all, the Lord desired that everyone should save himself. When the time arrived, this thoughtful man valued all the glory and the honor of this world as (being) nothing, while the beauty of this life appeared to him as smoke. Christ's love grew in him and filled his heart, as is the temple of Christ, and it became the purest repository for this holy spirit. Christ came into his mind as a gift and taught him. So he sent for his noble children and all twelve magnates high and low, and having assembled them around him, Nemanja began to instruct them in the following way: "My dear children, whom I have loved and brought up, let all of you know that God appointed me by his providence to rule over you; and that, in the beginning, I started ruling our country when it was in the most miserable condition; and with the help of God and our holy lady, the Mother of God, who has such power, I have neither rested nor have I become indolent until I set everything aright; and with the help of God, I increased your land in length and in width, as you all know. Until now, I have brought you all up as my own children and have taught you how to follow the Orthodox religion. 'Many foreigners stood up against me and assaulted me like a honeycomb full of bees,'[2] but, with the Lord's name, I opposed them and was victorious. So, you, my dear children, do not forget what you were taught and the Orthodox law which I established. When you follow it, you will have God and the holy lady Mother of God as your helpers, as well as my own sinful prayer. Let me, your ruler, leave in peace now so that my eyes will see the salvation which he has prepared for everyone in the world as a revelation to nations and as the glory to you, my flock.[3] I see that all human vanities will not survive death. Neither riches will remain nor glory will follow; death, having arrived, will annihilate everything. Therefore, we agitate ourselves in vain. The journey we are taking is a short one. '... For what is your life? It is even a vapor, that appeareth for a little time, and then vanisheth away.'[4] All vanities are really that way. Life is a shadow and a dream, and the agitation of all the people on earth is for nothing. As the books said: 'When we have gained the whole world, then we are moving to the grave where the kings and the beggars are together.' So, my dear children, let me go soon so that I can see Israel's solace." With these consolations, their good master and kind shephered talked to them, while they cried much and pleaded with him: "Do not leave us orphans, Oh Master; you baptized us, you taught us, and you educated us; oh, our good shepherd, sacrifice your soul for your flock. During the days of your rule, a wolf never seized a sheep from the flock which God bestowed on you. During all thirty-eight years of your rule, we have been taken care of and preserved and brought up, and we have not known any other master and father except you, our Lord."

Nemanja Abdicating, Advises His Sons

Like a father, the blessed old man advised them with wise words to cease their sobs and tears; and with God's will, he chose his noble and loving son, Stefan Nemanja, the son-in-law of Master Alexis, Greek emperor crowned by God. Nemanja introduced his son to them, saying, "You will have him instead of me. He is the tender branch which came from my body, and I am placing him on the throne of the state bestowed to him by Christ." He crowned his son himself, blessing him in as stately a way as Isaac did his own son Jacob. Then he began to teach him all the good things in his state. The old man taught the boy to be kind to the Christian people which were being given to him, to his flock saved by God, and then he told him, "My loving child, let this Israel of mine grow; take care of it and lead it as Joseph led the lamb." He commanded his son to pay attention to the churches and to those who serve in them, to obey with pleasure holy men and church servants, to honor priests and protect monks because they would pray for him so that he would not have to be reproached by God and the people. He blessed his other noble and loving son, Prince Vukan, and appointed him to be an archduke and gave him plenty of land; and having announced Stefan Nemanja, and having blessed Prince Vukan,[5] the kind father placed them before himself, saying, "'My sons, forget not my law; but let thine heart keep my commandments: For length of days, long life, and peace shall they add thee. Let not mercy and truth forsake thee: bind them about thy neck; write them upon the table of thine heart. So shalt thou find favour and good understanding in the sight of God and man.

Trust in the Lord with all thine heart; and lean not unto thine own understanding. In all thy ways acknowledge him, and he shall direct thy paths.

Be not wise in thine own eyes; fear the Lord and depart from evil. It shall be health to thy naval and marrow to thy bones. Honor the Lord with thy substance, and with the firstfruits of all thing increase: so shall thy barns be filled with plenty, and thy presses shall burst out with new wine.

My sons, despise not the chastening of the Lord, neither be weary of his correction; for whom the Lord loveth, he correcteth, even as a father the son in whom he delighteth.

Happy is the man that findeth wisdom, and the man that getteth understanding. For that merchandise is better than the merchandise of silver, and the gain therefrom better than fine gold. She is more precious than rubies: and all the things thou canst desire are not to be compared unto her. Length of days is in her right hand; and in her left hand, riches and honour. Her ways are ways of pleasantness, and all her paths are peace. She is a tree of life to them that lay hold upon her; and happy is every one that retaineth her.'[6] I am giving you this command: love each other and let there be no evil between you. Subject yourself to Stefan Nemanja and obey him whom God and myself have placed upon my throne. You, on the other hand, do not treat harshly your elder brother but honor him. He who does not love his brother does not love God, since God is love. Therefore, the one who loves God should love his brother. The whole law is about that, the apostles taught us that, the martyrs were crowned with it, and the prophets suspend their teaching on it and announce it. 'If ye be willing and obedient, ye shall eat the good of the land; but if ye refuse ... ye shall be devoured with the sword....'[7] To you, my loving sons, let peace be from the Lord and salvation be from our Jesus Christ. Let the spirit of God rest upon you, strengthening and protecting you from all visible and invisible enemies and instructing you in peaceful ways. Peace be with you, my noblemen and magnates. Peace be with you, my young ones whom I have brought up since you were born of your mothers. Peace be with you all, Christ's wise flock, bestowed on me by God and whom I preserved unharmed as the good shepherd by dedicating my soul for you. I am asking, therefore, my loving children, the rich ones and the poor ones, the old ones and the young, that you follow your father's teaching. 'Be subject to your masters with all fear....'[8] Make the churches famous so that they will make you well known. Obey the bishops, honor the priests, and be humble to the monks so that they will pray for you. Be just and loving to each other, do not forget charity. 'The grace of the Lord Jesus Christ, and the love of God, and the communion of the Holy Ghost, be with you all. Amen.'"[9]

Nemanja Sees Death Approaching, Parts with His Son

On the seventh day of the month of February, Nemanja, now in his honorable old age, began to feel ill. Thereupon the blessed old man, master Simeon, summoned me, an unworthy and humble person in all matters, and quietly began to speak with pure and sweet words: "My sweet child and the solace of my old age, '... attend to my words; incline thine ear unto my sayings...'[10]

'That thou mayest regard discretion, and that thy lips may keep Knowledge.'[11]

'My son, hear the instruction of thy father, and forsake not the law of thy mother.'[12]

'Forsake the foolish, and live; go in the way of understanding.

He that reproveth a scorner getteth himself shame; he that rebuketh a wicked man getteth himself a blot.

Reprove not a scorner, lest he hate thee; rebuke a wise man, and he will love thee.

Give instruction to a wise man, and he will be yet wiser; teach a just man, and he will increase in learning.

The fear of the Lord is the beginning of wisdom; the knowledge of the holy is understanding.

For by me thy days shall be multiplied, and the years of thy life shall be increased.'[13]

'Now, therefore, harken unto me ... for blest are they that keep my ways.

Hear instruction and be wise, and refuse it not.

Blessed is the man that heareth, watching daily at

my gates, waiting at the posts of my doors.'"[14] Having raised his blessed hands, he placed them on my sinful one and he started to cry with sadness. Bestowing on me his sweet kisses, he began again to speak: "My beloved child, the light of my eyes, the consolation and the defender of my old age. Now the time comes for us to part. Now the Lord is letting me go in peace so that what was said by Him will be fulfilled: '... for dust thou art, and unto dust shalt thou return.'[15] Do not grieve, my child, because of my parting; for from this goblet everyone will partake. If we part here, there we shall unite, where there is no more parting." Having raised his venerable hands and having placed them on my head, he said, "I bless you with a benediction. The blessed Lord will grant to you your salvation, but let him also give to you on earth forgiveness and mercy and the kingdom of heaven. Let him correct the course of your life, which originated with me; and may you have everywhere my indivisible, but nevertheless, sinful prayer." I fell prostrate before his venerable feet and spoke with tears, "I enjoy many great gifts from you, my blessed master, Simeon; forgetful of everything, I appear before you wretched and deprived of grace. I have become similar to mindless beasts of burden, joining them by being poor in good deeds and full of torments. Filled with shame, deprived of God's trust, condemned by God, bewailed by the angels, laughed at by the devils, accused by my own conscience, and ashamed by my wicked deeds, I have become dead before my passing away and have sentenced myself before the final judgment and eternal torments. I have tormented myself with doubt. Because of this, I, an incorrigible person, am falling before your venerable feet for the mercy of your honorable prayers which might bring about some alleviation for me in the days of the fearful coming of our Lord Jesus Christ." When the eighth day of that month arrived, he said to me, "My child, send for the spiritual father and for all the honorable old men at Mount Athos. Let them come here, for the day of my passing away is coming closer." His order was carried out, and the multitude of monks came like sweet smelling flowers blossoming in this holy desert. Having come to him, they received peace and blessing from each other; and he would not let them leave him, saying, "Stay with me, until you sing over my body and bury me with your holy and honorable songs." The blessed old man, from the seventh day until his death, tasted neither bread nor water; he partook only of communion with the holy and venerable sacraments of the Body and Blood of our Lord and our salvation, Jesus Christ.

Nemanja's Last Hours

On the twelfth of that month, I saw him getting ready for his departure and I said to him, "Oh, blessed master Simeon, behold, your gentle transition into your passing away is begun. I have heard already that you blessed your offspring, but give them now your last blessing." Then, having raised his hands, he began to speak with tears: "Oh holy Trinity, our God, I praise you, bless you, pray to you, and represent you. I give my third blessing to my offspring. God Almighty, the God of our fathers, of Abraham, of Isaak, of Jacob, and of our just race, preserve and strengthen it in the state I once ruled; and let the help of the holy Mother of God and my prayer, although sinful, be with them from now until eternity. I give them the old command: Love each other; if somebody strays from that which I established for them, let God's anger seize him and his descendants." To all that I said, "Amen." When the twelfth day of that month arrived, he said, "My child, bring me the icon of the holy Mother of God; my solemn promise is to expire in front of her;" and when the order was carried out and it was around evening, he said, "My child, a favor I ask: put the cover on me which is for my burial and prepare me in a saintly way, for I will be entering the grave. Spread a rug on the earth and place me on it, and put a stone under my head; let me lie here until God visits me and takes me from here." I did everything that he ordered. All of us, looking and crying bitterly, saw on this blessed old man an inexpressibly heavenly providence and godly concern. For even here he asked from God and God gave him everything in his state; until this hour he did not want to be deprived of a single spiritual matter, and God granted him everything. Verily, my dear brothers and fathers, that was a wonder to behold, that one before whom all foreigners and states feared and before whom they trembled looked like one of the strangers himself: poor, wrapped up in a cassock, lying on a rug on the earth with a stone below his head, bowing to everyone, causing pity and asking for forgiveness and blessing. The night having come, they all took leave of him and blessed him and went to their cells to perform their duties and to rest a while. I and one priest (whom I kept with me) stayed with him all that night. When midnight arrived, the blessed old man became quiet; he did not speak to me further. When morning came and the church singing was resumed, the blessed old man's face became immediately illuminated; and raising his hands to the sky, he said, "Praise ye the Lord. Praise God in his sanctuary; praise him in the firmament of his power."[16] I asked him then, "Father, whom did you see?" Having looked at me, he said then, "Praise him for his mighty acts; praise him according to his excellent greatness."[17] When he had said that, his holy spirit left his body; and he fell asleep in God. I then fell on his face, weeping bitterly for a long time; and having stood up, I thanked God that I saw the last days of this very noble man.

NOTES

[1] 1169-1196. The actual duration was 27 years. The different use of alphabet letters for numbers must have caused this inconsistency.
[2] Psalm 118:12.
[3] Luke 2:29-30.
[4] James 4:14.
[5] Prince Vukan was the oldest son of Nemanja who fought with Stefan Prvovenčani for the right of succession. The forthcoming is the scene of reconciliation between the two brothers.
[6] Proverbs 3:1-18.
[7] Isaiah 1:19-20.
[8] I Peter 2:18.
[9] II Corinthians 13:14.
[10] Proverbs 4:20.
[11] Proverbs 5:2.
[12] Proverbs 1:8.
[13] Proverbs 9:6-11.
[14] Proverbs 8:32-34.
[15] Genesis 3:19.
[16] Psalm 150:1.
[17] Psalm 150:2.

The Office for St. Simeon

Venerable Father, you found a good ladder to go up to the heights which Ilija found with the fiery chariot. Yet he did not leave others the way to ascend; while you, after your death, showed the way in your fatherland to those who were ruling. Oh heavenly man and angel on earth, the lighthouse of your fatherland: oh blessed Simeon, pray for the salvation of our souls.

Venerable Father, when you had to preach to your fatherland you were not silent; you talked with your pains, works, and tears, with which you led your flock to the true faith as to a tree nourished with your teaching. The angels were amazed, the people wondered, and the demons were terrified of your patience; of blessed Simeon, pray for our salvation.

With the force of the Holy Spirit, resembling your Lord, you abandoned your rule; and with the cross, you followed Christ and settled in Mount Athos. After receiving help there, your grave poured forth the salve of grace and made your sons happy before you. Oh, blessed Simeon, pray for the salvation of our souls.

Venerable Father, neglecting the kingdom on earth, you chose the riches of the holy words; and you decided to keep them. After leaving your wife, your children, and all the beauties of earth, you went to Mount Athos to serve God with the angels. Pray to Christ continuously for those who cherish your memory.

With the love of God you kindled your soul, you quenched carnal passions and created a spiritual life on earth, oh blessed Simeon.

With heavenly brightness, you gleam in the hearts of us remembering your illustrious memory; deliver your flock from all dangers with your prayers, oh most blessed Simeon.

...The superb creator of the heavenly firmament, oh Lord, the founder of the church, you strengthened me in your love, the end of all wishes, the fortress of believers, and the only lover of human beings.

You appeared before Christ as the toiler in the church of God, and you moved to Mount Athos, oh Venerable Father. Therefore, you gleamed with glittering good deeds as a holy man, pious Simeon.

Completely in love with the spiritual life, you were beyond world and flesh, oh pious one; you received the glory of wisdom and eternal communion.

Your body with its pains, oh Venerable One, blossomed into a well-cultivated ear of grain, your heavenly children are feeding upon it with love, celebrating your heavenly remembrance.

...Having left the kingdom on earth, you accepted the cross on your shoulders, dedicated yourself completely to God and went to Mount Athos to participate in the Holy Spirit. That is why you became a worker of miracles. Salve poured forth from your remains in the grave. Oh holy Simeon, pray to Christ, the Lord, to forgive the sins of those who honor you.

...With the streams of your tears, Father Simeon, you broke up the passions of the soul; and you became, oh most blessed one, the heavenly abode of the spirit.

With your faith you instilled a firm vigil, an always quiet rejoicing and a love which cannot be despised, oh most blessed father Simeon.

Having received grace, oh most blessed one, as a true worshipper of God, the grave with your remains poured forth the salve of mercy.

NOTES

[1] Elijah.

Sources

A copy of the original manuscript dating back to 1619 was preserved in the Monastery Studenica. It contained *Studenica Typikon*, Nemanja's *Charter to Studenica* and *The Life of Saint Simeon*.
P. G. Šafarik edited and published the manuscript in *Pamatky Drevniho Pisemnictvi Jihoslovanuv* in 1851 (first edition) and 1873 (second edition).
The manuscript is presently located in the library of the Czechoslovakian National Museum in Prague.

STEFAN NEMANJIĆ [THE FIRST-CROWNED]
(1165-1228) ruled: 1196-1228

Stefan Nemanjić, the First-Crowned, was the second oldest son of Stefan Nemanja and heir to the throne of Raška (1196-1228). He was the first Serbian ruler to adopt the title of king and the first to be crowned with a royal crown.

Stefan's literary heritage is modest in quantity but of high quality. He wrote part of the Hilandar Charter, which he issued between 1199 and 1206. In it he presented a highly poetic description of the Holy Mount and of his brother the monk--St. Sava.

Following the example of his younger brother St. Sava, Stefan also wrote a biography of his father, Stefan Nemanja. The two biographies differ in many details. St. Sava, a monk, was concerned with the monk Simeon rather than with the ruler Nemanja. The greatness of Nemanja, according to St. Sava, was not in ruling a country, but in giving up his earthly power and princely throne in exchange for the modest and ascetic monastic life. In fact, St. Sava's biography of his father gives an account of only Stefan Nemanja's last few years of life, from the moment he came to Mount Athos and became a monk until he died. On the other hand, Stefan, a ruler himself, portrayed Stefan Nemanja as a ruler and statesman. Unlike St. Sava, Stefan gave an account of his father's life from his youth to his death. Numerous lyrical and autobiographical passages add a poetic note to this otherwise systematic yet elaborate account of Nemanja's life.

Before his death, Stefan the First-Crowned became a monk and took the name Simon.

The Life of Stefan Nemanja

Oh, God's saints, bishops, priests, monks, my loved ones, and my brothers: I, Stefan,[1] unworthy sinner and grieved by his passing away, by him sired and educated, Stefan Nemanja, will relate to you the birth, life, and virtue of this saintly man (Stefan Nemanja). Since I was not present, I do not remember what happened at his birth, but I have heard it said that there was a big uprising in that part of the Serbian country and in Dioclea,[2] Dalmatia, and Travunia;[3] and that his father (my grandfather) was exiled by his brothers who were driven by devilish

greed. He retreated from their rebellion to his birth
place, Dioclea; and with God's favor and that of His holy
mother bore this saintly child (my father), whom God's
providence ordained to be the unifier of the annihilated
parts of his fatherland--to be the shepherd, the teacher,
and, moreover, the renovator of that which was wasted in
the place called Ribnica. Since in this country there
were also Latin priests serving in the church, he thought
it appropriate, with God's favor, to accept a Latin baptism. Returning to his father at the capital, he thought
it proper to accept a second baptism in the center of the
Serbian country, from the hand of the bishop and archbishop, in the temple of the most famous and supreme
Apostles Peter and Paul. He followed in this deed his
lord and shepherd Christ, as the writing said, "You said
that you sucked from both breasts, thus completing the
old and new testament."[4] His parents brought him up in
the right faith and in charity; and they looked at the
child, not knowing the secrets of heaven or the extent of
mercy which would be given to him to rule on earth and to
stay in heaven with the angels.

Nemanja is Ruling a Part of His Patrimony

During the time that Stefan Nemanja reached adoles-
cence and received a part of his patrimony--Toplica,
Ibar, Rasina, and the said rivers[5]--the ever adverse devil obstinately continued inflicting injuries on the just.
By enticing Stefan's brothers, he did not perceive in his
foolishness that a triple crown is woven around the head
of a just man in order to forbear temptation. The thought
of anger as a response to betrayal did not occur to
Nemanja; as he rejected the Devil's malice which incited
his brothers, he tried to please God and to do good deeds
before him. When the God-loving Tzar Manojlo[6] of Constantinople heard of the extraordinary wisdom, modesty,
and gentleness of this innocent man, he wanted to see
him. Having been near the Nišava region, he sent for
Nemanja to come and see him. Nemanja hastened to go to
Tzar Manojlo. Having seen Nemanja and having received
him with a sovereign embrace, he kissed him, admiring the
young man's wisdom; he honored Nemanja with the rank of
ruler and with different gifts. He then took a part of
his domain, Glubočica,[7] and gave it to Nemanja, saying,
"This is for you and your descendants forever; this

domain is to be shared neither with me, nor with my relatives." Let your mind not wonder at that, oh brothers, for sovereigns loved him with love worthy of sovereigns; and they increased his honors and ranks; and the other bishops obeyed him assiduously, because the Almighty Lord, Jesus Christ, loved him. Let it be known to every man, oh loved ones, that whoever loves Him with all his heart will succeed in everything. The sovereign loved the saintly man who knew his Master's love and whose heart was kindled with a godly fire to please God and to build temples for God's holy servants. With no delay, he began hurriedly to build a temple to the holy Mother of God in Toplica, his patrimony at the mouth of the river Kosaonica. He adorned the church with all things pertaining to it and established in it a congregation of monks with his honorable and God-loving spouse, Anna. He gave her the temple of the holy Mother of God to care for in every way, as well as the monks whom he settled in this holy place. She followed her duties with obedience and virtue, taking care of the temple of the holy Mother of God given to her by this holy ruler of ours. The wise man said about her; "A decent woman in her husband's home is worth more than a pearl and precious stones.[8] Pearls and precious stones are designed by the people on earth, but they are perishable, and the prophet declares that 'the fullness of good deeds are more valuable than pearls and precious stones.'"[9] She followed this by pleasing God in her husband's home.

Nemanja's Abdication and His Entrance Into the Monastery

After completing a prayer, Stefan Nemanja called his spouse, his sons, his bishop Kalinik,[10] the administrators and princes who were ruling the regions of his country, and the counts and military leaders, and he spoke to them: "My pious loved ones and my brothers, let it be known to you that I have longed to follow my Lord's command with heartfelt fervor since my youth, but my Lord did not deign it. Now the time has come for that which started long ago to end. I am bequeathing my country and my people to my successor who will rule over you on my throne. I have blessed him and you with my blessing as God blessed Job's descendants. Let him rule over you steadfastly." He stood up from his throne and gave the crown to his son with many blessings. He said then to

the bishop, "Come forward and complete my request," and
he received from the bishop's hand the monastic rank,
uniting himself and his spouse honorably to God. He was
called Monk Simeon, and she, as a nun, Venerable Anastasija. He went to the holy Mother of God, the benefactress of Studenica. He stayed there, living with
other honorable monks according to the rules of the holy
and pious fathers and in no way becoming indolent; and
he sent a message to the young monk who had left before
him for Mount Athos and whose name was now Monk Sava,
saying, "Let it be known to you, oh my loved one in
Christ, that what I begged for, what I wished for, and
what I asked for with all my strength and with all my
heart, my Creator granted me. Not because of my transgressions but because of his abundant and inexpressible
mercy and love for human beings, he deigned to bestow on
me what I was longing for--his honorable and angelic
monastic rank. Rejoice because of me and pray to your
Lord so that he could deign me, an unworthy person, to
come in at the twelfth hour to appear with you as the
worker in Christ's vineyard in order to receive his reward." Sava was glad and he thanked the holy lady Mother
of God, and added many prayers to his Lord with tears,
saying, "I thank you, oh Lord, that you did not abandon
those who seek you, trust in you, and toil for your
sake," and he wrote to Simeon saying, "Come, oh Master,
sincere servant of my Lord; come, oh the most revered
one. Your Lord is waiting for you and has prepared for
you all sorts of dwellings. Those who trust in him will
not be ashamed. '... Come, enter thou into the joy of
thy lord';[11] for unto those who love him, everything will
become well.'[12] Having received these words of mine, oh
my holy Master, hurry and take your cross and follow
Christ, making fast progress to the desired goal; and as
soon as you arrive hither, settle in the temple of the
holy Mother of God of Vatoped."[13] Having gathered there,
they lived with happiness of spirit, singing in the
church, being at vigils and praying honorably day and
night. The head of the monastery and all the brotherhood of Mount Athos, honorable abbots, and all brothers
and hermits came to visit him. Kneeling, they kissed
each other with tears, speaking to him about the improvement of the soul; and he asked them about their lives and
the rules of the monastic order. They were surprised and
miraculously amazed, and they spoke to themselves: "If
the merciful Lord and his most holy Mother did not choose

Mount Athos as the refuge of monastic guidance, they would have not brought him to us and made him leave his kingdom and his glory. Our Lord Jesus Christ, you chose to execute such awesome and most glorious deeds. We thank you for your graceful deed, which is now, occurring, because this saint sent his most beloved offspring ahead as a pure gift and a precious sacrifice; and then he hurried to come here himself. Oh, the Lord's mercy, the depth of his inexpressible love for humanity which can be seen among us: Verily, we understood how our Lord and the venerable Mother of God visited this holy place and our staying here for they brought to us our benefactor." This holy master of mine had arrived, and he did not neglect a single monastery which was here: beginning with the big ones and ending with the small ones, not a single one was left out, and each one was presented with all kinds of gifts according to its riches. He lit his lantern in all of them, and he left in them his brotherhood which has been there until this day.

NOTES

[1] Stefan Nemanja's immediate successor, Stefan Prvovenčani, Stefan The First-Crowned, ruled from 1196-1227. He obtained the title of King from Pope Honorius III in 1217. Although he was not Stefan Nemanja's oldest son, he won the right of succession. Stefan Prvovenčani married the daughter of the Byzantine Emperor Alexius IV Angelus (1203-1204).

[2] The Montenegro Littoral from Budva to Bar.

[3] The area to the interior of Dubrovnik around the town of Trebinje in Southwestern Yugoslavia. The official title of Stefan Prvovenčani was: The King of All Serbian Lands: Dioclea, Dalmatia, Travunia, and Hum (the valley of the Neretva river).

[4] This quotation could not be verified.

[5] Raška, Toplica, and Ibar have the same names as they had in the 12th Century.

[6] Manuel I Comnenus (1143-1180), the Byzantine Emperor.

[7] A part of today's region of Metohija.

[8] Cf. Proverbs 31:10.

[9] This quotation could not be verified.

[10] The abbot of Treskavica.

[11] Matthew 25:23

[12] Romans 8:28. A paraphrase.

[13] One of the monasteries on Mount Athos.

The biography written by Stefan Nemanja's son Stefan the First-Crowned is believed to have been written in the early 13th century. The manuscript was published and edited by Šafarik in his Book *Pamatky Drevniho Pisemnictvi Juhoslovanuv* in Prague in 1851 (first edition) and then in the revised second edition in 1873. The manuscript is located in the French National Library in Paris.

"Praise to St. Simeon"

What hymn of praise could my poor lips
offer in your praise, O Venerable One?
Because my intelligence is inadequate,
I implore you, O my Master,
for I am confused
and unworthy to dare to praise
your virtues;
nevertheless, I am one of your own, my Master,
and I offer praise to you:

Rejoice, my Master,
my beginning and end
and my holy guardian.
Rejoice, O good Shepherd
of the reason-endowed flock
which the Lord acquired
through His precious blood.
Rejoice, O Flower of bright colors,
you have armed yourself
with the power of the Cross
and with invincible armor
in order to defend your flock
from the herd of wolves
which attack it at all times.
Rejoice, O Teacher of the New Testament,
teaching in the manner of Moses
yet following the footsteps of Paul,
whose teaching you have excellently implanted
in our mind.
Rejoice, O Venerable One,
a leader of the aged,
protector of widows,
and a benefactor of the poor.

Rejoice, O Knowledge and Strength of the young
and Teacher bringing improvement.
Rejoice, O Helper in battles,
rejoice, O Victor over the hostile barbarians,
rejoice, O Leader
which leads his children and subjects
to heavenly shelter
and settles them on the spiritual meadow.
Rejoice, O Precious Ornament of Bishops
and Righteous Wreath which does not wilt.
Rejoice, O Co-Dweller with the apostles
to whom you are equal in teaching and preaching.
Rejoice, O Competitor of the martyrs,
their co-sufferer who receives the same praise as they.
Rejoice, O Vigilant Eye of the monks
and wonderful teacher,
an ineffable [living] typikon.
Rejoice, O Comfort of the ascetics living in the wilderness
and serenity of those who lead a monastic life.
Rejoice, O Correction of us sinners,
rejoice, O Purger of sins,
Rejoice, O Calm Harbor of those who are tossed by the waves.
Rejoice, O Breaker of the chains of sin,
Rejoice, O Road leading to heaven.
Rejoice, O Bridge leading to heaven.
Rejoice, O Unfathomable Wellspring.
Rejoice, O Paradise everlasting, splendid and majestic.
Rejoice, O Flower of faith of the heavenly garden.
Rejoice, O Reason-endowed fortress of your nation.
Rejoice, O Fruitful Vine
from which our joy pours.
Rejoice, O Ripe Vine
from which a sweet unfermented wine is flowing
which cures us from inebriation with sin.
Rejoice, O Saintly Master,
Rejoice, I repeat,
rejoicing always near the throne of your Lord.
Yet, O Venerable One, remember me,
your sinful servant Stefan.

Sources

Church Slavonic text published in

Ćorović, Vladimir. *Svetosavski Zbornik*, II. Srpska
 Kraljevska Akademija. Beograd. 1939.
Schafarik, Pavle. *Památky dřevniho pismenictvy
 Jihosluvanuv*. Praha. 1851.
_____. *Geschichte des serbischen Schriffthums*.
 Prag. 1865.

PK

Serbian translation published in:
 KFD;
 SSK, I.

DOMENTIJAN
C. 1210-after 1264

Domentijan was a major figure in medieval Serbian literature. He was a monk at the Monastery Hilandar and a contemporary of St. Sava. In fact, he accompanied St. Sava when the latter visited the Holy Land. He was much respected by the royal court in Raška, as well as by the monks on the Holy Mount. Teodor's account of his troubles, recorded on the pages of John Exarch's *Hexameron*, which Teodor was copying at Domentijan's request, contains many references concerning Domentijan and his character.

Domentijan's authorship of a biography of St. Sava, written c. 1253, and one of St. Simeon Nemanja, written c. 1264, is uncontested. He wrote St. Sava'a biography at the request of Uroš I, the ruler of Raška. It is a work giving an account of St. Sava's life, yet it is also an apotheosis of monasticism. Domentijan's style is characterized by fluent narration, panegyric diction, abundance of theological and mystical elements with an emphasis on a spiritual and clearly monastic point of view. This work was written by Domentijan while residing in St. Sava's Kelia at Karyes (capital of the Mt. Athos monastic community).

For his biography of St. Simeon, Domentijan used material from works of other authors. Thus, it is established that he "borrowed" 438 lines from Stefan the First-Crowned's biography of Stefan Nemanja; one third of his own biography of St. Sava; and in the Panegyric to St. Simeon, he used a few lines from Ilarion's Panegyric to St. Vladimir.

It may be concluded that Domentijan was essentially a hymnologist who wrote biographies of two Serbian saints but, in fact, glorified monasticism and Christianity.

The Life of Saint Sava

Rastko's Birth

The most merciful God, who has always listened to those who love Him and granted the petitions of those who respect Him; who heard Abraham and Sarah and granted them Isaac in their old age, as He had promised; who also heard Zachariah and Elizabeth and gave them John the

Baptist, the divinely-radiant ray who preached the true Sun of the world, Christ the Lord; then [too], Joachim and Anna [who] in accordance with the promise gave birth to the Guardian of our Life, the All-Pure Mother of Christ our Lord; [He], according to the words of the apostle, "Jesus Christ [who] is the same yesterday and today and for ever,"[1] heard after many years the pure prayer of those righteous ones [Stefan Nemanja and his wife Anna], too; and He did for them what He had done for the aforementioned righteous people.

And then the God-loving Anna conceived in her womb; and, according to the will of God, gave birth to a son, an off-shoot which sprouted nicely from the healthy root, through whom his parents received divinely-radiant joy, and [for which] they offered thanks to their Benefactor Who had not ignored their prayers. And after his conception they did not come together in their bedroom; but, as they had promised God, they remained in [chastity] until the end of their life. And they baptized their God-given son in the name of the Father and the Son and the Holy Spirit; and they named him Rastko,[2] who indeed was to grow in stature through pious good deeds; and, furthermore, not he alone, for he was to lead his native land toward great piety [thereby] completing the pious works initiated by his parents who indeed received through his birth a message from the Holy Spirit that he was given to them by God as a gift. They always experienced great joy on his account [and] they continuously offered thanksgiving prayers to the Lord; they brought him up piously in true faith and chastity, recognizing in him a messenger of God. They built palaces in which he, the light-bearer of God, lived and grew up and radiated the grace of God [elected], to enlighten his native land.

His parents, who felt a great love for him, used to visit him often; and they marvelled very much at him and pondered anxiously [about his future, saying]: "What shall become of this child which has been sent to us by God?" They entrusted him to God's providence and they taught him [to read] the holy books. And as often as they visited him, they felt an ineffable joy in their soul [for] the grace of God which was upon him foretold to them mysteriously, through the Holy Spirit, joy forthcoming, depicting for them future endless bliss in the Lord God; and they obtained endless joy through the prayers of him to whom they had given birth.

After [his parents] had brought him up in great love and true faith, and after he had been taught to love God and to be virtuous, they gave him a part of their kingdom to rule and to enjoy along with his servants. They were unaware of the mysterious plan God had for him, but, instead, they hoped that he would reign on the throne of his father; and they [therefore] did not reveal to anyone the grace of God which they had noticed upon him at that time, but they treasured it in their hearts, saying, "What plans has the Author and the Seer of mysteries for him?"

And he, the true sapling of God, was immune from vainglory from his early youth; and, from his childhood, adhered to the Lord through prayers and fasting, according to the saying of the prophet: "Blessed is the man who fears the Lord,"[3] whom the Lord shall elect from his youth and with whom He shall work together.

After he had spent some seventeen years in his father's house, inspired by the Holy Spirit he believed the word of the Lord, which He spoke with His truth-speaking lips: "He who loves father or mother more than Me is not worthy of Me,"[4] "And he who does not take his cross and follow me is not worthy of me."[5] And he understood that this life is transitory, turbulent, and worthless, and that it passes quickly; and, having seen with his spiritual eyes the futility of life and the inexhaustible riches prepared for the righteous who love Him,[6] and deeming earthly glory worthless, he abandoned the earthly kingdoms, and said with joy: "Let me first fulfill that which the Lord has said, for it was the Lord Who had said, 'seek first His kingdom and His righteousness, and all these things shall be yours as well'"[7]' and he armed himself with the Holy Spirit, and "having girded his loins"[8] with the knowledge of God, virginal chastity, and great endurance, he prepared himself with sincere prayer and spiritual love to become a lamp burning for Christ.

Because of his sincere faith in Christ, the Lover of Love Himself lived in his heart, in accordance with the word of the divine apostle who had said "in Whom are hid all the treasures of wisdom,"[9] this treasure was hidden at the bottom of [his] heart, because God Himself said: "Blessed are the pure in heart, for they shall see God,"[10] for He Himself is hidden in the heart of the one who loves Him and believes in Him. For this reason he gave up the earthly kingdom to acquire that precious treasure on earth, by which he enriched himself, his parents, and, also, his native land, burning with the Holy Spirit and continuously praying to the Lord to show him the road to salvation.

NOTES

[1] Hebrews, 13:8.
[2] The name derives from the verb *rasti*, meaning *to grow*.
[3] Psalm, 112:1.
[4] Mt., 10:37.
[5] Mt., 10:38.
[6] I Cor., 2:9.
[7] Mt., 6:33.
[8] Eph., 6:14.
[9] Col., 2:3.
[10] Mt., 5:8.

Rastko's Departure for the Holy Mount[1]

And the Lord brought to him an able monk from the Holy Mount. The humble youth offered him a very warm welcome and inquired of him about the Holy Mount, and this one told him wisely and piously all about the life of the saints of the Holy Mount. After he had heard so much from him [the monk], he became fond of the counsel which was sent to him by God, and he understood the voice which had reached him from the Holy Mount and from the All-Holy Mother of God, whom he accepted as his Mediator and the Trustee of his life. He offered many fervent prayers to the All-Pure Perpetual Mediator for the salvation of the human race, speaking thus, "O, All-Pure Mother of universal life, who provided unsolicited mercy, entreat Thy Son, my God and Creator, to 'send out His light and His truth to lead me and to take me to Thy Holy Hill and to Thy dwelling,'[2] which Thou hast prepared for those who love Thee; and make me worthy to 'come into Thy house'[3] to the sanctuary of God and to God who is the joy of my youth; and I shall 'bring Him the offerings of thanksgiving and lay down my vows before the Lord, that which my lips uttered,'[4] in order that I may become an example to my native land and to all those who love Him."

After he had ended his prayer and strengthened himself with hope in the All-Pure One, he gathered the God-fearing people with whom he was to follow Christ, left the province in which he had resided, and came to his father. His parents received him with great joy, and there was a great feast in honor of the arrival of their dearly beloved son; and after some time had elapsed, he said to his parents, "My lords, allow me to go to that part of the country"--he named it--"for my hunters have informed me that the hunting is very good in the mountains of that country." And his parents told him to go.

However, owing to the fact that he was captured by Christ long before and hit by the arrow of love for the One by Whose love he was wounded, he armed himself with the Holy Spirit, made the sign of the life-creating cross in his heart, and told the Lord, "Set my feet on the road of peace, that I may step on it and walk in pursuance of Thy truth throughout my life, always, now and for ever and unto ages of ages, amen."

And after he had received the blessing of his parents, he left, experiencing joy in the Lord his Saviour, taking shelter in the mountains like a bird, in accordance with the saying of the ancestor of God [Christ], David: "Oh Lord, who shall sojourn in Thy tent? Who shall dwell on Thy Holy Hill? Who walks blamelessly, and does what is right, and speaks truth from his heart,[5] he shall receive blessing from God and grace from God his Saviour." This, exactly, happened to him; for he became fond of the ascetic life from his very youth, in a way similar to John the Baptist, the Forerunner of Christ. For, according to the evangelist Luke, he, too, "went to the wilderness and stayed there till the day of his manifestation to Israel."[6] And this one was selected by the Lover of Love and the Lover of Mercy, Christ, even from the womb of his mother, and brought to His Holy Mount where he remained till the day He called him to enlighten his native country. During the time that he lived on the Holy Mount, he addressed his Creator with love day after day: "O Lord, I love the habitation of Thy house, and the place where Thy glory dwells."[7] And beholding Him with a radiant mind and touching Him with his spiritual hands, he exclaimed, "Upon Thee I have leaned from my birth; Thou art He who took me from my mother's womb";[8] "O Lord, guide me to the road of Thy mercy, for Thou art the Guide of those who go astray and the Haven of those tossed by the waves; and all our forefathers set their hope on Thee, and they were never disappointed; yea, do likewise with me, Thy servant, according to Thy mercy; look upon me and be merciful unto me; show the radiance of Thy face to Thy servant and teach me Thy statutes that I may uphold Thy words and I shall live for ever."

And the most merciful God heard the prayer of the one who loved Him and brought him to the Holy Mount and settled him in the house of St. Panteleimon, the Russian monastery.

NOTES

[1] Mount Athos, located at the Chalcidic Penninsula, in the northeastern part of Greece, near Thessaloniki. It has been the center of Orthodox monasticism for over a millenium. The first monastery was built in 963, yet the hermit type of monastic life started there several centuries before that.
[2] Psalm 42:3 [adapted].
[3] Psalm 66:13.
[4] Psalm 66:13 [adapted].
[5] Psalm 15:1-2.
[6] Lk., 1:80 [adapted].
[7] Psalm 26:8.
[8] Psalm 26:8.

The Search Party Finds Rastko the Holy Mount

After he had lived there for a while, chosen soldiers, sent by his father, and many others from the territory of Thessaloniki, dispatched by the emperor Master Isaac,[1] [arrived] and brought a letter in which the protos and all hagiorites[2] were strictly ordered not to allow him to stay with them under any circumstances.

When they arrived, they found him in the house of St. Panteleimon. They were very glad because [they had found] him, and they offered thanks to the Lord for this, hoping to take him back to his parents [for which they would] receive a generous reward from their master, his father, as well as some recognition. They, therefore, guarded him with great care to prevent him from escaping somewhere again.

It so happened that the holiday of Sunday was approaching, and on Saturday, on the eve of Sunday, he prepared a great feast and treated the servants who came after him very warmly, as well as the residents [of the monastery]. With the honorable abbot of that monastery, however, he made an agreement that as soon as they [the soldiers] retired, the bells should start ringing to invite everyone to the church service and the celebration of that holiday. The vigil service was very long and the watchmen, who sat down during the chanting of *kathismata*,[3] being very tired, fell asleep. At that time, the lamb of Christ [Rastko] implored his Shepherd with a profound and sincere supplication: "O Gracious One Who lovest man and Who lovest soul, hear my prayer, let the cry of my heart reach Thee[4] and incline Thine ear to me, and rescue me speedily[5] and be my Helper and Protector; let Thy mercy descend upon me; hide me under the shelter of thy rich mercy; O, my Joy, 'deliver me from my persecutors,'[6] 'and rescue me speedily; save me in the house of refuge, for Thou art my fortress and my refuge.'"[7]

And the lamb of Christ, whom the Lord the Ruler of Heaven had marked for Himself, could not be injured by beasts; and neither the love of parents, nor vainglory, nor anything else could separate him from the love of Christ. During the time he stayed there, he began to do good deeds; and he donated a great amount of gold for the upkeep of St. Panteleimon Monastery.

NOTES

[1] Isaac Angel, Byzantine Emperor, 1185-1195 and 1203-1204.

[2] Dwellers (monks) of the Holy Mount. The term derives from 'Αγιον Οσος , meaning *the Holy Mount*.

[3] A type of Orthodox church hymn. Faithful are allowed to sit during the chanting of this type of hymn, whereas they are supposed to stand during the chanting of the others.

[4] Psalm 102: 1 [adapted].
[5] Psalm 31:2.
[6] Psalm 142:6.
[7] Psalm 31:2-3 [adapted].

Rastko Becomes a Monk

The most merciful Lord Who is "near to all who call upon Him,"[1] and Who grants the petition of all who respect Him, sent advice from His divine wisdom into his heart and he [Rastko] summoned one of his servants and made him put on his [Rastko's] garment [and] told him to stand in his place till the end of the church service. And he [Rastko] entered the altar area at the end of the First Entrance,[2] and there he gave his offering to the Lord, soaking the holy altar with many and bitter tears; and he found himself in the situation [in which was] his Lord when the soldiers guarded the tomb of His All-Holy body. Protected by His invisible might, he was able to slip by the soldiers who were watching him, but did not recognize him. And after he went past them, he entered the tower, locked himself therein, and offered praise to his Saviour Who had bestowed such great mercy upon him; and he bowed before the Lord his spiritual and corporeal knees, offered prayers, took the [monastic] vow before his Lord, sheared his hair, and put on the garb of monks; and when the church service ended, at the end of night and the break of the dawn, they [the soldiers] did not find the one they had been watching.

Then the abbot and all the monks found themselves in serious trouble; and there was great agitation in the monastery, for they [the soldiers] harrassed, abused, and beat up the monks, demanding that they deliver their Master. Seeing such cruelty, commotion and abuse of the monks, the young man who possessed divine wisdom, called from the tower to the leader of the soldiers and addressed [all of them]: "Here I am, do not search for me and do not abuse the monks; you see the purpose of my coming to the Holy Mount has been accomplished." He then showed to them his shorn head and the monk's garb he had on; and he handed them his [shorn] hair, telling them, "Take this to my parents as evidence from me." And after they had bewailed their Master, they returned full of bitterness because they had accomplished nothing.

NOTES

[1] Psalm 145:18.

[2] Also referred to as the Small Introit: Procession from the altar area into the nave of the church and back to the altar. Rastko, obviously, joined the procession and followed the hieromonk or hiermonks into the altar area.

Sources

Church Slavonic text (manuscript): *MHM* #505.

Church Slavonic text published in *PK*; *ŽSS*.
Serbo-Croatian translation published in: *ISSK*; *KFD*;
   SSK.I;
Domentijan, *Životi sv. Save i sv. Simeona*. Lazar
   Mirković, tr. Beograd: Srpska književna zadruga.
   1938.

Rastko's Departure for the Holy Mount Athos

One of the servants informed his [Rastko's] parents: "Your son, the one whom you love, has left the world in order to follow Christ." This message shocked them and they asked themselves: "Is this true or not? Did our beloved child really leave us? Did our favorite despise our great love and care? What shall we first tell our heavenly Benefactor concerning this ineffable sorrow which has suddenly befallen us? How shall we begin the lament caused by the departure of our beloved child? What kind of road is the one he became so fond of that he took it without asking our consent?" Hurriedly they dispatched their dukes and noblemen in all directions to look for their beloved child.

After having visited many provinces of the Greek country, they found him on the Holy Mount at St. Panteleimon's house,[1] in the Russian monastery, to which he had moved and joined the other monks, taken the cross of the Lord on his shoulders, and put on the holy angelic [monastic] rank.

When those who were dispatched had seen all this, they returned and told of all that had happened with the wise youth. When his parents heard the words of those who were sent [to look for Rastko], they, as well as their close friends, were seized by sorrowful weeping; and they and their subjects put on mourning garb. There was great lamenting and distress all over their country, such as had never been heard or seen before; the holy churches intensified their praying, and everyone was seized by the fear of God and humility. And some people, inspired by the Holy Spirit, sang mournfully songs they had composed about the departure of the young man filled with divine wisdom.

NOTES

[1] Russian Monastery on Mount Athos.

Stefan the First-Crowned's Letter to St. Sava

After you, the Venerable and Saintly one, left us, our country was defiled by our sins and was afflicted by bloodshed. We became the prey of foreign peoples. Our enemies ridiculed us and our neighbors mocked us because of our transgressions. When foreigners came, they indeed devastated the homeland of the Saint [St. Simeon] and what the Venerable One had gathered in one piece, they split asunder as their prey. Some [people] were cut down by weapons, others were taken prisoners. Some were deprived of all their belongings and thereby exposed to utter poverty. And later, when by the help of God those [foreigners] were defeated and had left, another foreigner came; one named hunger, worse than those who preceded him. He took his prey, larger than the one taken previously, and he had no pity whatsoever on our people; he killed without arrows, pierced without spears, cut without swords, murdered without clubs; and he pursued although he had no legs, he grabbed although he had no arms, he stabbed without knives, moved about unarmed yet sowed many corpses, in accordance with the sacred Old Testament where it is said [that] when the hand of the Lord killed the first born [sons] in Egypt, in revenge for His firstborn Israel, there was no home in all Egypt where there was no mourning and no dead.[1] In the same manner, because of our sins, our whole country was crowded with dead: they filled the yards, the houses, the roads, and the paths. And because of our sins, the gravediggers were unable to bury them but somehow laid them down in the holes dug to store wheat.

Notes

[1] Exodus, 12:30.

Sources

Church Slavonic text (manuscript): *MHM*, #505.
Church Slavonic text published in *ŽSS; PK*.
Serbo-Croatian translation published in: Domentijan, *Životi sv. Save i sv. Simeona*. Lazar Mirković, Tr. Beograd: Srpska književna zadruga. 1938.

Saint Save Became an Archbishop and Secured the Serbian Independent Church

Holy Master Sava, having spent some time in Mount Athos in the monastery he had built, departed for the East to the venerable Emperor in Constantinople, Master Theodor called Laskar. Sava was instructed by God to do this, and he accepted God's advice in his heart. Sava was received by the Emperor with great honor. This pious Emperor loved Sava immensely and wanted to participate in Sava's holiness because the Emperor knew that Sava was brought up piously and that, loving God, he left the world and wanted to serve God in a saintly way. The Emperor kept Sava many days at his place while holy Sava took care of monastic affairs. Then Sava put in a word to the Emperor about his fatherland, saying, "I am sad and grieved, Emperor, that my country does not have her own archbishop. There are, moreover, many countries around my fatherland dominions of our state, which God's teaching has not reached. If pleases your Imperial Majesty, I would like you to instruct the patriarch to consecrate an archbishop from one of the brethren who is now with me. My country could then be enlightened by him and your state would thereby be glorified." The Emperor, answering the Venerable One, said, "I will fulfill your God-inspired and pious request with great happiness, God willing; and I would like to see the one to whom your pure soul will elect for that sanctification." The brethren who were with the Venerable One were invited before the Emperor, and none of them pleased him. The Emperor said to the Venerable One, "None of them is worthy of such sanctity as you with your God-given saintliness and glory." The Venerable One answered, "Neither am I worth of such rank." The Emperor said, "I had reports even before your arrival that your saintliness was equal to that of the apostles, and God showed you to me as being worthy; do not object." The Venerable One responded, "I am not prepared for this; where shall I find such money to pay for such expenses which church law requires?" The Emperor then answered, "I will provide from the palace of my kingdom all that your saintliness requires, only do not deny the grace of the Holy Spirit; it is not becoming for you to oppose God's command. The Holy Spirit has let me know that God entrusted you with the flock of your fatherland, as nobody else could better guard your flock than you, true shepherd." The Venerable One felt burdened by his honor but he could not disobey God's and the Emperor's command, and he said to the Emperor, "Let God's will be." The Emperor told the Patriarch all about the Venerable One and about his fatherland. And the honorable Patriarch German, having accepted God's and the Emperor's advice, shared their will. On a festive day, the Patriarch put on his vestments according to the rites of the Great Ecumenical Church with many metropolitans, archbishops, priests, and deacons being present. The venerable Master Sava was to be initiated and then ordained as an archbishop by the hand of German, the holy and ecumenical Patriarch, and by the command of the Emperor Master Theodor Laskar of Constantinople. Miraculous God glorified His holiness by having selected Sava already in his mother's womb and in his youth, and bestowing on him holy deeds on Mount Athos.

The abundance of his saintliness also became known to the Emperor in the East, and Sava was deigned with the grace of the Holy Spirit in its plenitude. The pious Emperor consecrated that day in honor of the newly-ordained Archbishop Master Sava. There was a joyous celebration with plenty of alms for the people. The Emperor paid proper homage with precious gifts to the honorable Patriarch, the metropolitans, archbishops, priests and deacons, and the whole clergy of which the great ecumenical church consisted. The Emperor not only donated what was customary, but went beyond that as befitting the honor of his great kingdom and his beloved Sava.

As we mentioned above, the Emperor gave away much gold from his palace on that day with the desire to be honored by Sava's saintliness, and that is what happened. The honorable Patriarch had the holy one (Sava) during this time at his side and Sava spent as much time with the Patriarch as he did with the Emperor, discussing God's teaching and spiritual uplifting, as well as sacrificial examples in the saintly and apostolic tradition. And this holy Patriarch also became very fond of Sava, bestowing magnanimously upon him spiritual joys and God's love, as well as his patriarchal vestments and array. Mules with red embroidered saddles symbolizing the Emperor's honor were also given. As the Heavenly Father of His own will gave power over heaven and earth to His own Son to rule, so this holy father, being the father of the whole ecumenical church, gave to his newly-ordained, spiritually-reborn son all the necessities of his sublime rank along with his most venerable scepter and all-heavenly power. The Patriarch then wrote the following to all believers: "The most venerable Patriarch of the whole state, German, has ordained Master Sava to be the Archbishop of all Serbian and coastal lands. I am sending him as my beloved son to all the people who live in the diocese of the Orthodox Christian religion of my spiritual care. Let him have a diocese like mine extending over all cities and countries; let him rule over metropolitans, bishops, priests and deacons according to Canon Law and the rank; and let him teach everybody in the name of the Father, Son and Holy Spirit. Let all of you who are Orthodox Christians in Christ obey me in this."

Sources

Domentijan. *Životi sv. Save i sv. Simeona.* Lazar Mirković, tr. Beograd. Srpska književna zadruga. 1938.

ATANASIJE
13th Century

He was a disciple of St. Sava, yet very little is known of him. His hymn to St. Sava has been preserved in Domentijan's biography of St. Sava in the part describing the return of St. Sava's remnants from Trnovo, Bulgaria, to the Monastery Mileševa in Raška. On that occasion, according to Domentijan, Atanasije spoke these words. It is quite possible that Domentijan created this hymn and attributed it to Atanasije, yet it is generally believed that Atanasije, in fact, did deliver it orally and, consequently, that he was its author.

Eulogy to St. Sava
[in Domentijan's *The Life of Saint Sava*]

O divine, O beloved,
O sweet and most holy voice,
O God-glorifying Sava,
You have firmly promised
to be with us until the end of this world,
O divinely-adorned Sava,
and we, your beloved children,
who have you as our strength
and our divinely inspired hope,
are rejoicing now.
O what a wonder, brethren,
more splendid than any other wonder,
awesome and filled with ineffable amazement.
O, great is the power of God
and ineffable are His wonders,
so that one who loves God
and abides by His will
cannot be destroyed even by the grave
and the earth cannot imprison him.
Moreover, even during his lifetime
the sea itself
was obedient to him,
and after his death,
death did not affect
his God-bearing Body.
But, moreover, like an aromatic lily
it grew on the fragrances of his virtues
which blossomed from his youth,

and, as the prophet said:
"his body did not undergo decomposition."[1]

NOTES

[1] Acts, 2:31.

Sources:

[This text is part of Domentijan's *The Life of St. Sava*]

Church Slavonic Text: (manuscript) *MHM*, #505.
Church Slavonic text published in *ŽSS*.
Serbo-Croatian translation published in: Domentijan.
　　Životi sv. Save i sv. Simeona. Lazar Mirković,
　　tr. Beograd: Srpska književna zadruga. 1938.

SILUAN
14th Century

Siluan, the author of a hymn to St. Sava included in this Anthology, has not been positively identified. There are two writers from two different historical periods, both of them named Siluan and both of them monks at the Holy Mount. Either of the two could have been the author of this hymn. One of them lived in the 14th and the other in the 15th century. Very little is known about either of the two. We believe that the author of the hymn was Siluan from the 14th century.

A Hymn to Saint Sava

By escaping from glory
you have found glory, O Sava,
there,[1] whence came glory to the nation.
You have preferred the light of faith
to the light of the [mundane] kingdom,
and thereby illumination came to the whole nation.
Superiority of mind overshadowed supremacy of rank,
thereby you achieved in actuality a goodness
which surpasses understanding.

These words of praise to Sava
were put together by Siluan.

NOTES

[1] A reference to Mount Athos.

Sources:

Church Slavonic text (manuscript): *MHM*, #249; #250; #427.
Church Slavonic text published in: Ćorović, Vladimir. "Siloan i Danilo II," *Glas Srpske kraljevske akademije*, cxxxvi, drugi razred, 72. Sremski Karlovci. 1928.
Serbo Croatian translation published in *KFD*; *SSK, III*.

TEODOSIJE
13th-14th

Teodosije, one of the most talented medieval Serbian writers, was a hieromonk at the Monastery Hilandar on Mt. Athos. Surrounded by the beauty of nature and the mystical atmosphere of Hilandar and Mount Athos, this monk-poet transferred some of that beauty and serenity into his literary works, characterized by its poetic quality.

Teodosije was an original and prolific writer. In the period between 1292 and 1310 he wrote a *Common Canon to Christ, St. Simeon Nemanja and St. Sava*, *The Life of Saint Sava*, "Encomium to Ss. Simeon and Sava," a *Common Canon to Ss. Simeon and Sava*, another *Canon to Ss. Simeon and Sava*, *The Life of St. Petar of Koriš*, *Office for St. Sava*, and *Office for St. Petar of Koriš*.

Teodosije's biography of St. Sava, compared to Domentijan's, is written in a less ornamented style. It is relatively free from mystical and theological elements, and it shows the author's mastery in the choice of biographical details narrated.

The Life of Saint Sava[1]
Saint Sava Having Become an Archimandrite, Returned to Serbia with Nemanja's Remains

When Sava arrived at his monastery Hilandar, he summoned to him Nikolai, who was at the time bishop of Erisa. Bishop Nikolai performed the holy service with many priests, ordaining him (Sava) that day as a holy hierodeacon. On the following day, Sava was ordained as a hieromonk.

Bishop Nikolai and Sava were very happy afterwards in the company of monks and many poor people. All who were present--the bishop, priests, and the poor--were presented with gifts and then left for their homes. The holy one, as a newly ordained hieromonk, blessed the abbot and the monks, bidding them all peace, and then returned again to his cell of silence in Karyes.[2] Later he went to the Protos[3] in order to be blessed, since he had fulfilled the will of the prior and also of God. The Protos met him and received Sava as warmly as he would have his own son, blessing him like a father; and, while kissing Sava's newly-ordained hand, the Protos placed it on his own head. Sava was splendidly received at the

Protos' table, and after enjoying their conversation, Sava retired to the cell where he was spending his life as a monk.

In order to obtain the provisions necessary for the monastery, Sava chose to go to the town of Salonica. Upon arriving in the town, he entered the holy church of Christ's suffering great martyr, Demetrius. He kissed the martyr's grave, and then, after smearing himself with the holy myrrh which always flows from Demetrius' body, he returned to his own monastery, Filokalia.[4] He had given much gold for the erection of that monastery, and for this reason, those living in it considered him to be its founder. He went after that to visit with the then holy father, Archbishop Kostandi.[5] Bishop Kostandi wanted to see Sava because he had heard much about his virtues. It just happened that the aforementioned Nikolai, the Bishop of Mount Athos, came at that same time and told Kostandi everything about both blessed Sava and his father, the very venerable Simeon. Nikolai said that God honored Simeon with a miracle by welling up the myrrh from Simeon's holy remains. The archbishop, having heard this, marveled; and praising God, he praised the honor of the holy one and rejoiced in His love. When the distinguished day of the holiday arrived, the archbishop desired to perform the holy services himself. With him were Nikolai, the Bishop of Erisa, Bishop Mihail of Kasandria,[6] and Demetrius, the Bishop of Adramera.[7] They asked the Venerable One to be their assistant, and he, obeying their request, joined them in the bloodless[8] service and participated in Holy Communion. Then the archbishop and the bishops blessed Sava, ordaining him as archimandrite, and they blessed the hip vest which he would now wear at all times while serving the holy liturgy. After leaving the church together, they partook of the corporal table as well as the awesome and the holy. And so the holy one parted kindly from the bishops, and having accomplished all the necessary things for the monastery, he took away with him a glass with the myrrh from the holy remains of his venerable father and sent it to his kind brother, King Stefan. He wrote down on paper all that God had done with the Venerable One, and he sent it to Stefan together with the holy myrrh. He returned again after that to Mount Athos.

After the emissaries came to the Serbian kingdom, they gave King Stefan the glass with the holy myrrh and the letter. This lover of Christ stood up with great happiness and, while bowing, kissed the guests. After reading the letter, he understood the sequence of God's favors because of venerable Simeon, his father; and he was overwhelmed with many tears, thanking God for many wonders and praising His mercy. He then called his bishops and all the noblemen who were there, and he ordered the letter to be read aloud so that all of them could hear. After hearing about the mercy of God's wonders, which had occurred because of his venerable father, all of them were amazed; and they praised God for it.

I would like to tell you now about the hatred between the brothers, but I hesitate, filled with shame. Let us not condemn the brothers for the one who was the cause of the hatred, the one who in the beginning, exalting with pride, said to himself, "I will place my throne on a cloud, and I will be like the Almighty."[9] Because of this, he was overthrown from the sky with all the rebel forces. "The father of envy, hatred, and lies, the devil, ... who has been the murderer from the beginning,"[10] the one who began to envy the distinction of the first man, Adam, and who rose with hatred against the latter because of his conceit and his desire to be equal to God, caused Adam to be expelled from paradise. The evil one contrived much defamation....

Then he created hatred between the two brothers. The great Prince Vukan hated his brother, the King Stefan, because of their father's blessing. Venerable Simeon, when leaving for Mount Athos, appointed his son Stefan in his place as the ruler and the king of the whole Serbian country. The father strengthened him with his prayers and his blessing, saying: "...Let the one who blesses you be blessed and let the one who curses you be cursed. Let the sons of your father bow to you, and let your arms be upon the shoulders of your enemy; you will be the master of your brothers."[11] After his father's departure, Vukan, overpowered by stubbornness and enslaved by envy, said to himself, "The day of my father's death is approaching, and then I will have my revenge."[12]

After the holy old man passed away, Vukan opposed his brother in many different ways. He never stopped hating and trying to harm his brother, King Stefan. He accepted the help of many foreign peoples; and prompted by wicked advice, he rebelled against his brother frequently, always wishing to injure and remove Stefan from his throne. But although the great Prince Vukan gathered many foreigners together and rose up in many battles against the impregnable fortress of King Stefan, founded on prayers and the paternal blessing, it was said that whenever he attacked, his forces became scattered, and he was not able to realize his intentions in any way. He was put to shame and routed by Stefan many times. Even with all his foreigners, he was always turned back. Finally, filled with shame and seized with fear, they retreated to their strongholds blocking the narrow road passages behind them from Stefan. During this hatred and persecution between the two brothers, the Serbian country was overwhelmed with great scarcity and distress. It became uninhabited because of much plunder and bloodshed. The country began to perish from hunger because the land was not filled, and many people went away to foreign countries. The devil, the sower of malice and the hater of goodness from time immemorial, reaped a bountiful harvest. The Christ-loving brother, King Stefan, wrote thus to blessed Sava, who carried God in his heart, asking and saying, "Oh, master and holy father, so dear to my heart and soul. Listen to the voice of my lament, attend to my sighs and do not disdain this request. Favor us by sending here the holy and myrrh-giving remains of our holy and venerable father. Have pity on us and bring them yourself from the foreign country to your fatherland, so that with your holy prayers, our fatherland will become spiritually strengthened and all of us will be blessed. Since you have left us, 'our land has been defiled by our lawlessness and is now perishing in blood';[13] foreigners have conquered us, our enemies have mocked us, and with our hatred against each other, we are a disgrace and a spectacle of contempt for all. Perhaps, with your holy prayers and your arrival, the most merciful God would have compassion for us by uniting our scattered people and destroying our adversaries."

    This godly man, having heard this and being the follower of God's mercy, was grieved in his soul about it; and, exerting himself in behalf of his brother, wanted to fortify him through unshakeable faith in Christ. Sava then spoke to his pupils: "Whatever you ask as believers will be granted to you."[14] In the same way, Sava also hoped that all he asked from God would be given to him, as he himself had amazed others with miracles such as producing the flow of myrrh from his venerable father at Mount Athos. Thus, he boldly hoped that God would glorify and celebrate him again before his own sons and people in the Serbian country. For the appearance of wonderful miracles, through which "God is illustrious among his saints," Sava took with him some of the venerable men from Mount Athos, all those who shone like the sun in their admirable lives. He and these saintly men took the holy and myrrh-giving remains of his saintly and venerble father, and undertook the journey to their fatherland, so that they could announce truthfully in the western country that they were witnesses in the East, on Mount Athos, of God's wonders which glorified His worshippers. After their return to the eastern regions, they planned to relate again what they had seen happening in the West, in the Serbian country, so that God would be praised with one voice by everybody and would be glorified in all his counsels.

He informed his brother, the king, about his journey with the holy myrrh-giving remains of their father, and asked him to prepare for them a suitable welcome. When the good Christ-loving Stefan heard this, he became full of incomprehensible happiness; "'What shall I give to God,' he said, 'for everything God has given me?'[15] I was considered worthy to have seen my father on Mount Athos. There I saw the holy and myrrh-giving remains of my saintly and venerable master and father, and with him my brother, my very soul, whom I have been longing to be with for many years, whom I carried in my heart without seeing, and whom I will be meeting now and whose inconceivable love I will enjoy to the full glory of you, oh kindhearted Lord of us all. You took men away from us and created angels from them; and now you send them back to us because of your kindness. I do not know how to praise you, my Christ....' I am earth and ashes,'[16] and I can only admire your mercy." With his bishop, venerable monks, and all the clergy, he set out immediately with his nobles and arrived at the border of his and the Greek state. There, they [Stefan and his retinue] met respectfully the most honorable and holy relics of his venerable father, filling the air with the pleasant aroma of the incense streaming from the censers. They [Stefan and his retinue] received the relics by singing psalms and hymns suitable for the memory of his venerable father. Honoring his relics with tears and joy, kissing them lovingly, looking at them with admiration and touching them with their faces as if to receive sanctification, they raised them [the relics] and carried them.

They all kissed and kindly embraced holy and saintly Sava with the same tears, without being able to thank those holy men who came with him from Mount Athos for such a magnificent treasure that they brought to the Serbian country. The visitors admired, for their part, the fullness of King Stefan's love and his great modesty, for he did not spare the king's purple cloth, which I say was of little beauty compared with his own honorable head which he lowered into the dust. Stefan bowed to the feet of the venerable guests, asking them all to receive his prayers and his blessing. They all said after David: "'His seed shall be mighty upon the earth; the generation of the upright shall be blessed:'[17] accept our blessing." And so, all having blessed God, they consoled themselves and rested together.

NOTES

[1] The third and the youngest son of Stefan Nemanja, Rastko (1175-1235), who became a monk of Mount Athos under the name of Sava. He was the first Archbishop of the autocephalous Serbian Church (1219).

[2] One of the monasteries on Mount Athos founded by the Nemanjić dynasty.

[3] A monk selected as the administrative head of the monastic community at Mount Athos.

[4] A monastery in Thessalonica.

[5] The Bishop of Thessalonica during St. Sava's stay on Mount Athos.

[6] The place situated on the Gulf of Thessalonica. Bishop Mihail was under the Jurisdiction of Archbishop Kostandi.

[7] Bishop Demetrius was under the jurisdiction of the Archbishop of Thessalonica at the time of St. Sava's stay in Mount Athos.

[8] As opposed to the original sacrifice.

[9] Isaiah 14:14.

[10] John 8:44.

[11] Genesis 27:29.

[12] Genesis 27:41; a free rendition.

[13] Leviticus (3 Mojzes) 18:27; a paraphrase.

[14] Matthew 21:22.

[15] Psalm 116:12.

[16] Genesis 18:27.

[17] Psalm 112:2

Sources:

Teodosije's *The Life of St. Sava* was one of the most popular medieval biographies, and it existed in full or abbreviated form in more than sixty versions. They were very popular in Bulgaria and especially in Russia. Daničić published and edited a manuscript in 1860 which was based on a version from The National Library in Belgrade. According to Daničić, this version is from the 15th century. One page was missing from Daničić' manuscript which was later incorporated from another version and published in 1865. One of the oldest copies of the manuscript is the one from 1336 by Teodul which was believed to be a copy of the original. It was located in the Monastery Hilandar on Mount Athos for centuries, and the moved to the National Library in Belgrade, where it disappeared during the First World War.

The Office for St. Simeon
[Excerpt; Tone 5]

Rejoice, O blessed Simeon;
after having enlightened yourself
with the knowledge of the Holy Trinity,
you enlightened your nation
with faith in the Holy Trinity,
and strengthened by the power of the Cross
you eradicated soul-mortifying heresy;
you erected holy churches
and you taught us to worship the Son Incarnate
Who is equal to the Father and to the [Holy] Spirit;
adorned with justice and mercy
and enriched with many pious deeds,
now you are in the company of the bodiless powers [angels];
together with them entreat Christ
to bestow His rich mercy upon our souls.

Rejoice, God-loving Simeon;
afflicted with the true love of Christ the Lord,
Who was incarnate of the Virgin
and Who for our sake sojourned in this world,
you took dislike of the beautiful things of your kingdom
and having estranged yourself from your people
and your children,

you won the admiration of your people
by your retreat from the world;
you shamed the evil spirits by your humility;
you provided great joy for the angelic hosts;
and now, sharing abode with them,
enlightened with the divine light
and enjoying the most splendid radiance,
O Father, entreat Christ
to bestow His rich mercy upon the world.

O Venerable Father, O wonderful Simeon,
after you had come to Mount Athos,
and after having become a competitor to its ascetics,
in your old age you practiced asceticism like a young man;
after you had regenerated your soul
with abstinence and prayers,
and irrigated it with the rain of your tears,
and sown and raised in it the grace of the Holy Trinity,
and after you had become its beautiful abode,
now your tomb, around which your people stand,
manifests itself filled with [the grace of] the Holy
     Spirit
by the issuance of healing myrrh;
entreat Christ with your prayers
to bestow upon us His rich mercy.

Sources:

Church Slavonic text (manuscript): *MHM* #161; #241; #249.
Church Slavonic text and Serbo-Croatian translation
    published in: Trifunović, Djordje, et al. *Srbljak*,
    4 volumes. Beograd, 1970. [Text in Volume I].

Canon to St. Simeon

1

With the zealousness of [Elijah] the Tishbite
you have uprooted shameful heresies;[1]
pray that my shameful thoughts
may perish together with them
through your prayers to Christ,
that I may with boldness praise you,
O Simeon, the godloving and ever-blessed one.

When you were enlightened
by the light of the most radiant Trinity,
O venerable Father,
having abandoned the darkness of heresy,[2]
you led your nation from the darkness of ignorance
into the light of the knowledge of God,
O Simeon, the godloving and ever-blessed one.

Strengthened by faith in God,
you defeated heretical insolence
and raised the banner of the church of the faithful,
teaching your nation
to worship Christ the Son, consubstantial with the Father,
and the Holy Spirit, who is of equal glory,
the indivisible Trinity
in one Divinity.

3

The hatred of your brother and [his] envy of your honor
put you into prison:
there in the image of St. George,
God's angel, Father,
appeared to you
[and] broke your heavy fetters
and led you out of the deadly dungeon, O Simeon.

The lamentable and conceited one
revolted because of your love for God,
he, who by his nature is similar to Cain,
attempted to commit another fratricide
by gathering a host of foreigners against you,
O Simeon,
whom you,
being strengthened by God,
have defeated
by your lance.

One who set a trap for you
was himself entangled in it
when God took His revenge upon him;
and, as He once drowned Pharoah,
He drowned this one in the river water,
thus appropriately glorifying you, O Father,
because you have trusted Him.

In nature and deeds you proved to be another Abraham
by adorning yourself with generosity and faith;
being obedient to God,

you left your native country and relatives
and in foreign lands
you lived in God-pleasing manner,
because of which He allotted to you the lot of Abraham;
and now, having received it, you rejoice;
and the tomb where your remnants rest
pours the healing myrrh,
making happy your sons
who sing praises to you;
O Simeon, godloving Father,
pray Christ the Lord
to grant forgiveness of sins
to those who lovingly respect
your blessed memory.

4

With the illumination of the indivisible light
of the thrice-illumined Trinity, O Simeon,
you enlightened your nation;
and, reinforced by it, O Father,
you chased the heretic wolves, exclaiming:
Glory to Thy power, O God.

Having strengthened your soul, O blessed one,
with the unity of Faith and hope,
and by the bond of love,
you proved yourself to be
of a generous and righteous heart,
and because of it the True Light enlightened you
and joy - light's consort.

Having conceived a longing for an inconceivable beauty
which you experienced in your life,
you left your spouse and children,
you forswore wealth and throne, O Father,
and thereby you inherited the ascetic life as your cross,
and you died for Christ together with your son,
    exclaiming:
"Glory to Thy power, O Lord."

5

During your life in the earthly kingdom
you were famous for your wealth and power,
and having exchanged this for an ascetic life,
you became similar in poverty to the poverty of Christ
    the King,
who became incarnate on the earth,
who, therefore, enriched you with many gifts.

You exchanged the vanishing and transitory
for the stable and eternal,
and the temporary and decaying
for the heavenly, O Father,
there rejoicing in triumph together with angels;
pray, O Simeon, for us,
the ministrants of your memory.

O what a goodly trade was yours,
O how wise was your exchange:
with the decaying wealth
you bought the eternal one,
you exchanged the mundane power
for the heavenly kingdom,
where rejoicing now, O Father,
pray to Christ for us.

6

Instructed by heavenly wisdom, O Simeon,
and having rejected the mundane as unreal,
you settled in the wilderness, observing fasts
and always confessing to God;
clinging to Him with love,
you spent your life joyfully.

In your pre-monastic life, you were experienced in
    military art,
and you won many victories over your enemies;
in your monastic life, too,
with your humility and prayers,
you spiritually
defeated the hosts of devils,
O Father Simeon, who art praised for both (achievements).

Gladdened by an inconceivable glory,
by the joy of the beauty of paradise,
and by the hope of the light of spiritual joy, O Father,
you lived faithfully in the wilderness with your son
and, therefore, together with him, O Simeon,
you rejoice eternally with Christ.

Kondakion

Having become fond of the angelic life here on earth,
you abandoned wordly power and the world,
and through fasting, you followed Christ, O Simeon;
like an apostle you led to Him those who love you,
exclaiming: "Love God for He loves us."

Ikos

You humbled yourself
before the crucifiction and death
as the One who was humbled for our sake;
by fasting, you carried the cross
and thereby you defeated the one
who boasted that he would found his throne on clouds.
Because you fought valiantly against the insolent one,
you were amply glorified by Christ,
the great Benefactor.
Standing now in front of Him,
as a lover of your nation, remember it;
preserve your flock intact
against attacks of enemies;
by anointing with myrrh
identify your people;
[and] by your prayers, O Simeon,
make the enemy of the soul fly away from them;
lead them like an apostle
and exclaim aloud to those you love you:
"Love God for He loves you."

7

In your old age, you made the youthful decision
to take up the narrow path
which leads into the spaciousness of paradise;
[and] you came up to the Tree of Life,
where now you rejoice in bliss;
pray, O Simeon, to Christ
that we may also come there.

On earth, O Father,
you gave to God by giving to the poor;
He, now in heaven, has given you
the lot of the venerable and righteous ones,
thus making you their peer on earth
and their equal in heaven.

Abiding by His commandments,
illumined by Christ's love,
you abandoned the shimmer of the world;
[and] having fled from worldly commotion into the desert,
Father, and having increased your knowledge of God,
you acquired an unworldly serenity.

8

Fleeing from material beauty
as from a dream,

and wishing to acquire the spiritual one,
you entered the Holy Mount, O Simeon;
and having your son as a leader in spiritual endeavours,
you were not betrayed in your expectations.

Longing only for that which leads you into life [eternal]
you by-passed worldly beauty
and thereby acquired a non-worldly inheritance;
from there, enlighten the souls of those who sing hymns
    unto you;
O Simeon, you who have been awarded
an ineffable illumination.

Due to the virtues of your son,
you have found the Sun on earth;
illumined by his words, O Father,
you received honor more luminous than stars.
Standing together in front of Christ,
O Fathers, pray for us who honor your memory.

9

You were found to be great in generosity and goodness;
you proved to be the heir of many inconceivable treasures,
like a son who inherits his father's treasures,
O most generous hand,
O supreme gift
of Christ who glorified you,
O Father Simeon.

To her who gave birth to one of the Trinity,
you erected a splendid church
where your myrrh-exuding relics
offer healing to those who approach them with faith,
in which we, your descendants,
glorify Christ
by honoring your memory.

Burdened with sins
and stooped by passions,
we appeal to you, O Father,
asking to be relieved from both;
being an elect of Christ the Lord,
help us by your prayers to rise
from those falls injurious to souls.

Now your holy memory
illumines those who honor it,
for, O Father, you lived a saintly life
and were found worthy of receiving the light of the
    saints;

make us worthy to receive a part of your honors
and do not reprimand us for asking so much.

NOTES

[1] Bogomilism is one heresy meant here. The other may be Roman Catholicism (see footnote 2).
[2] Nemanja never belonged to the sect of the Bogomils; thus, this cannot be a reference to Bogomilism. He was, however, first baptized according to the Latin rite in Ribnica. It is, therefore, possible that under the term "heresy" one may understand it to mean Roman Catholicism.

Sources

Church Slavinic text (manuscript): *MHM* #126; #161; #241; #249; #254.
Church Slavonic text and Serbo-Croatian translation published in: Trifunović, Djordje, et al. *Srbljak*. 4 volumes. Beograd. 1970. [Text in Volume I].

The Life of Petar of Koriš
[Excerpts]

Having had the opportunity to become acquainted with the sacred books, having meditated upon the commandments from the Gospel, and having listened to the Lord as He said there: "Who loves his father or mother more than me, he is not worthy of me,"[1] he conceived the idea to leave his parents, and if, by going somewhere, he could find someone serving God, to stay with him and to serve Him [God]. With this [idea], he occupied his thoughts. And soon his father was called by God, and his mother understood her son and was aware of his intention to leave; and, as mothers do, she embraced him, and crying, she told him, "Do not leave your mother, my child; have pity on my widowhood; have pity on the misery of your sister [who is] still a girl. You know that, except for God, I have only you and her as my soul's consolation. Do not leave me, I beg you, lest I die weeping because of you, [and] then you will be responsible to God for having caused my death. I am not compelling you to eat meat or to get married. Stay and live as you please, only do not leave me." And he, feeling pity for her wretched maternal heart and being detained by her many tears, did not leave at that time, but immediately assumed the care of the household previously handled by his father; and, being in this respect obedient to his mother, he worked, subjecting himself to her with respect, yet imposing upon himself even stricter fasting; because of this, he was mockingly given the nickname "lenten food-eater." Next to his skin, he wore sackcloth; and no one knew of this but his mother. Because of this, his mother's grief for him increased, for she saw the flower of his youth wither because of his fasting. However, being afraid that he might leave, she let him live as he pleased. Then his mother expired, too, and having left her daughter to him, she went to the Lord. And he, having paid the respect due his mother through tears, funeral psalms, and required rituals, distributed to the poor everything he found in the house; and, having unburdened himself, he intended to go where he had wanted to from the beginning; but the youthfulness of his sister, as well as the fact that he had no one with whom to leave her, detained him. Moreover, when he asked her: "Do you want to get married, my sister?," she, being fond of chastity and being quite upset by this question, replied to him: "If you yourself avoid marriage, why do you try to impose it upon others? By the living God and by your living soul, [I swear] I will not do that [get married] nor will I leave you. 'Your God is my God, too; and where you go and settle, I too will go;'[2] and as you live, observing fasting, I, also, will live with you; only do not leave me." And after having pleaded with her a long time to get married and having failed to persuade her, he said: "May the Lord's will be done."

Having left the village and his father's house, the Venerable One received the angelic rank through monastic vows in a church located above that village, [dedicated] to the holy and First among the Apostles, Apostle Peter, [by the laying of hands] of an elder who lived there. There he built a hut for his dwelling and another, not far from his, for his sister; then the brother and sister lived by serving God through prayers and fasting, eating vegetables only. Their friends, acquaintances, and relatives marvelled at their strange retreat and their lives devoted to God; they visited them and brought them necessary things [for life]. The Venerable One protested very much against this, and the visits of many people made him quite uneasy; he, therefore, said to his sister, "It would be better for us to live far from our people, so that we do not see either their joys or their sorrows." She answered, "As you wish, Master." They got up and went to a different area, to [a place] known as Altin, where they continued their ascetic life, once more near a church [dedicated to] the holy and First among the Apostles, Peter. However, there, too, they were unable to conceal themselves from visitors because of their pious deeds.

The Venerable One, having listened to the biographies of the ancient Fathers, and being wholeheartedly ready to put his strength on trial by more difficult [ascetic] tasks, wished to settle in some wilderness where no one would know him, but the cordial ties to his sister obstructed him. He deplored this fact very much, saying, "Oh, what a great bother this woman is to me!" And once, when he could take it no longer, he left her alone and escaped. And his sister, sensing this, abandoned her hut and went after him. And having reached a high mountain located near the city of Prizren, above the village known as Koriš they stopped there to rest from their tiresome travelling, for his sister was exhausted and, thereupon, fell asleep. And the Venerable One wished to find even a cracked stone in that mountain into which he could enter and inside of which, God willing, he would spend the rest of his life in solitude. And he thought of how miserable and inconvenient it was for one to live in the desert with a female; and he, therefore, said to himself, "It is better to give preference to God than to one's sister; and it is more expedient to sadden her temporarily rather than to offend God."

Having arisen to pray, he spoke while making prostrations: "'Lord, Thou knowest all things!'[3] And Thou knowest the longing of my heart for Thee; [and] that because of my love for Thee, I am now leaving my sister alone in this wilderness; for I wish to serve Thee, my God, without being bound by anything. In accordance with Thy benevolence, direct me there, where I might lay a foundation for my penitence, sincerely repenting my evil deeds. I declare my willingness and give my promise; Thou shouldst give me endurance to live in this wilderness until the end of my life. I also pray for this handmaiden of Thine, my sister: may Thou so decree by Thy benevolence and may Thy good angels lead her there, where, in pleasing Thee by her penitence, she might spend her life. Do not overlook, O Lord, that for Thy sake she lived in celibacy, chastity, and fasting. Protect her by the shelter of Thy power from all visible and invisible snares of the devil so that I, too, Thy servant, may rejoice and exult in her salvation." And having then made the sign of the cross over her honorable head, he left her while she was asleep, pouring forth a river of tears at the parting; and, having entered the wilderness, he hid himself from her. And awakening from her sleep and not seeing him, she looked for him, calling his name; and having failed to find him even after a prolonged search, she realized that he had fled from her as he had originally intended. And crying bitterly on the mountain and tearing apart her heart with her sorrowful lament, she cried, "Woe to me, this is my end. Woe to me, my brother-master and my leader to salvation. Woe to me, my sweet light of which I am now deprived. Where did you go after you abandoned me? Our mother entrusted me to you, and you left me mercilessly alone in the wilderness; you deserted me and fled away. Woe to me, what is my reward for sleeping and what is my gain; O, why did I not, who was already covered by sweet agony, end my life then, thus, avoiding being trapped by this agonizing affliction? And now, alive though I am, I am lost finally and irrevocably. Woe to me, the miserable one; what should I do, where should I go? O, holy mountain of God, please let me meet my death here. Be you at least merciful to me; accept me here and may my grave tie me to you for ever; for I do not want to return to dwell in the world, nor does it befit me to live without being able to look at my brother and master."

This she said and many other things which would move one to tears; and thus, crying and lamenting, she went to another [part of the] country where people did not know her; and there she spent her life in celibacy and chastity, in fasting and prayer, as she had learned from her brother. And having thus well pleased God, she expired. And when the Venerable One received later the news of her death, he thanked God and rejoiced, because he, too, was always praying to God for her salvation. This, then, was what happened to the sister of the Venerable One.

NOTES

[1] Mt., 10:37.
[2] Ruth, 1:16.
[3] John, 21:17.

Sources:

Church Slavonic text (Manuscript): *MHM* #479.
Church Slavonic text published in *PK*.
Serbo-Croatian translation published in *ISSK*.

TEODORE
13th-14th CENTURIES

A protegé of Domentijan, he left some information about himself in an inscription in the copy of John Exarch's *Hexameron* which he had copied at the Domentijan's request. His problems with the authorities at the Holy Mount when he was beardless were later solved, for, apparently, his bear must have grown and he was able to become a monk. (One should know that beardless persons, as well as women, have been excluded from the Holy Mount. No beardless person was allowed to become a monk or had the right to come and stay on Mount Athos.)

Some literary historians claim that Teodor is no other than the famous medieval Serbian writer Teodosije. Their theory is that Teodor, after becoming a monk, took the name Teodosije.

A Scribe's Introduction

This book was written at the request and through the support of our holy, venerable, and divinely-inspired hieromonk Domentian, who at that time was an elder at the Monastery Hilandar; he was a saintly book-lover and, in the true sense of the word, a great lover of God to whom honor was given in heaven by God Himself and His angels because of his ardent love for both the most gracious Source of Grace and His holy testimony, as represented in the sacred books.

I was beardless when I came to the Holy Mount, and I stayed there one year before I was found by this Christ-loving (spiritual) father of mine; he learned from me that I was able to copy sacred books and the two of us alone, save for the presence of God, conversed and planned as to how, God willing, we would do this.

At this time, the persecution of beardless ones[1] by the Protos[2] and monks of the Holy Mount began; and they expelled many of them from the Holy Mount, myself included. I went to the city of Thessaloniki where I remained for half of a year. My blessed (spiritual) father, who incessantly blazed with the Holy Spirit, did not abandon the desire of his heart, but came and led me out of the city of Thessaloniki; and, being endowed with divine wisdom, he brought me back to the Holy Mount;

and, after having invoked the Lord's name, the two of us
began [to write] this book. When I had written the
first half, the envious devil implanted [an evil thought]
into the heart of one of my enemies who falsely accused
me before the Protos. The Protos then sent several envoys to my [spiritual] father on my account. This truly
good [spiritual] father and benefactor of children did
not allow me [to go] alone, desiring to prevent my being
mistreated and punished as others were. Thus, when the
holiday of the Dormition of the Mother of God arrived,[3]
my [spiritual] father took me and [we] went to the Council of Holy Fathers. We found the Protos in a very bad
mood and [he was] hostile towards me, being incited by
my enemy. My [spiritual] father was interrogated about
me by the Protos who greatly distressed my [spiritual]
father on my account; yet the Lord God was with my
[spiritual] father and He did not allow him to be completely humiliated by the Protos. I stood there and
looked at my [spiritual] father's sad face and I was
overcome by an intense sorrow; and, believe me my
fathers and brethren, it seemed to me as if I were at
the Second Coming [the Last Judgement] and as if I were
told what punishment I was to be given. But because of
the mercy of God and the prayers of my [spiritual[
father, God saved me from all those punishments which
the Protos intended to inflict on me. Finally, however,
I was sentenced to be expelled once more from the Holy
Mount. Yet, even then, my [spiritual] father did not
abandon me; he sent me to an estate belonging to Hilandar, where I, guided by the Lord and directed by the
prayers of my [spiritual] father, completed the other
half [of this book]. My [spiritual] father did not deprive me of his blessings and all my effort was rewarded. May the Lord not deprive my [spiritual] father of
His mercy here or in eternity.

NOTES

[1] Beardless men, as well as women, were not allowed
to reside on the Holy Mount; and there were several persecutions of the beardless in the course of the history
of the monastic republic of Mount Athos. This area is
still prohibited to women.

[2] The chairman of the Council of Karyes, composed of
twenty monks (at present); i.e., one representative from

each of the twenty monasteries situated on Mount Athos.

[3]Also referred as the Feast of the Falling Asleep of the Mother of God. It is celebrated on August 15 (Old Style Calendar), or August 28, according to the New Style Calendar.

Source

Church Slavonic text published in *ZIJK*, kn. 1. 1902.
    Serbo-Croatian translation published in *ISSK*; *KFD*; *SSK II*,

NIKODIM OF HILANDER
+ 1323
14th Century

Nikodim was a monk at Hilandar in the fourteenth century and, later, a Serbian Archbishop. His biography is included in *The Lives of Serbian Kings and Archbishops* by Danilo II and his disciples.

Nikodim's autobiographical note was inscribed in a manuscript in the year 1318 or 1319.

A Visit to Constantinople

There was a great dispute, inspired by the ancient evildoer [the devil], and there was a serious quarrel between my Master, the illustrious King Uroš,[1] and his brother King Stefan;[2] and at that time, I was the abbot of the Monastery of the Holy Mother of God at Hilandar, which is on the Holy Mount. At the request of both brothers, as well as the National Council of Serbia, I was dispatched to New Rome,[3] the Imperial City. At that time, the empire was ruled by the right-believing Emperor Master Andronikos[4] and his son, Emperor Master Michael,[5] and his grandson, Emperor Master Andronikos;[5] the ruler of the ecumenical throne[7] was the Patriarch of Constantinople, Master Nifon.[8] At that time, happened to be there also the Patriarch of the Holy City of Jerusalem, Master Athanasios,[9] I saw and paid my respects to the ineffable treasures which are [stored] there and [watched] the liturgical order [as observed] by those diligent men who officiated at the service in accordance with the tradition of the Holy City of Jerusalem, according to the typikon of St. Sava the Desert-Dweller. I received spiritual reinforcement, consolation, and the counsel that the two brothers, as well as the entire Serbian land, should live in peace and unity. When I was elevated to this holy and great throne of St. Sava [Nemanjić], I always thought of the efforts and work of blessed and holy men; and, moreover, abiding by the teachings of our leader and teacher, St. Sava, I tried to implement them as much as it was possible. I, therefore, sent [the envoys] to the Imperial City to the Monastery of St. John the Forerunner, and this typikon was brought to me, and I translated it from Greek letters into our language.

NOTES

[1] Dragutin, 1276-1282.
[2] Milutin, 1282-1321.
[3] Constantinople.
[4] Andronikos II, Byzantine Emperor, 1282-1328.
[5] Michael IX, Byzantine Emperor, 1294-1320.
[6] Andronikos III, Byzantine Emperor, 1328-1341.
[7] The throne of the Ecumenical Patriarch.
[8] Nifon I, 1310-1314
[9] Athanasios III.

Source

Church Slavonic text published in *ZIJK*, i, 1902. Serbo-Croatian translation published in *ISSK*.

JEFIMIJA
c. 1348 - c. 1405

Her secular name was Jelena. She was a daughter of Vojihna, the ruler of the province of Drama, and the wife of Uglješa Mrnjavcević, another medieval Serbian feudal ruler. She was a tragic and majestic figure in Serbian history. Raised at the court of her father, she was apparently well-educated and a talented person.

The tragic events in her life seem to have been the source of inspiration for her literary compositions, which were engraved on the golden backs of icons or embroidered on shrouds and church curtains rather than written on parchment or paper. The premature death of her infant son Uglješa, which came shortly after the death of her father Vojihna, signaled the beginning of the tragedies which were to befall her. The child was buried together with his grandfather in Monastery Hilandar on Mount Athos, the Greek territory at a distance from the province of Ser, where Jelena resided at the court of Uglješa, her husband, and prohibited to all women. The young mother was unable to visit the grave of her son and to mourn there. Instead, she engraved her lament for her beloved son on the back of the diptych (two-panelled icon) which Teodosije, the Bishop of Ser, had presented as a gift to the infant Uglješa at his baptism. The precious piece of art, valuable because of the gold, precious stones, and beautiful carving in wooden panels, became priceless after Jelena's lament was engraved on its back. The beauty of that lament is in its simplicity and its restrained and dignified, yet quite evident, maternal sorrow. The young mother admits that she cannot help grieving. What was intended to be a prayer for the deceased child became the confession of a mother unable to conceal her mourning. Engraved on the icons depicting Mother and Son, Jelena's lament for Uglješa immortalized the sorrow of all mothers mourning their deceased children.

The year 1371 brought another tragedy to Jelena's life. Her husband Uglješa, together with his brothers Vukašin and Gojko, gathered their armies in order to try to stop the invading Turkish forces. They met the Turks at the River Marica; and in the ensuing battle, the three brothers Mrnjavčević, as well as the major part of their armies, were killed. The Turkish invasion of

Raška and other Serbian feudal provinces was postponed for less than two decades, but at a very high cost. Jelena's personal tragedy was augmented by the national tragedy. At twenty-two, she was already a widow--helpless and unconsolable. She had to leave the court in Ser and move to Kruševac, the capital of Raška at that time, where she accepted hospitality of the court of Prince Lazar Hrebeljanović and his wife Milica. Shortly before moving to Kruševac, Jelena became a nun and took the name Jefimija.

While at the court of Lazar Hrebeljanović, Jefimija, who seems to have been excellent in the art of embroidery, embroidered a curtain which she sent to the Monastery Hilandar as her gift. The text embroidered on the curtain is not Jefimija's original composition, but a combination of passages from the prayers before Holy Communion by Simeon, the New Theologian, Simeon Metaphrastos, and St. John Chrysostomas. It is a large, beautifully embroidered, and ornamented curtain which is still treasured in the Monastery Hilandar. Its dimensions are 1.4 m. by 1.18m.

The tragic Battle of Marica in 1371 was but a prelude to the fateful confrontation between the invading Turkish forces and the Serbian warriors, led by Prince Lazar, which took place in 1389 on the Field of Kosovo. The defeat of the Serbs marked the beginning of almost five centuries of Turkish occupation of Serbian lands. Jefimija's host and protector, Prince Lazar, was beheaded at the order of Bayezid. Once more, Jefimija's sorrow was augmented by national tragedy through the loss of her beloved and respected friend Lazar. Once more, she expressed her grief through art: she embroidered a shroud for Lazar's coffin. On that 0.99m. by 0.69m. shroud, she embroidered a poetic text of original creation in which she addressed the saint-martyr directly rather than God, as was customary. This shroud was completed in 1402; and in 1405, shortly before her death, Jefimija embroidered an epitaphion which was 1.70m. by 1.11m. In the text embroidered on this epitaphion, the Mother laments her Son, indicating the possibility that Jefimija was actually thinking again of her own deceased son while working on this embroidery.

Jefimija's literary compositions are characterized by her use of the first person and by her expression of concrete and personal sorrow and anxiety rather than abstraction.

This unhappy mother and unfortunate wife, who was able to convert her sorrow into beautiful art, died c. 1405.

The Lament Over the Dead Son Overcome by Her Montherly Ways

Small icons, but a great present,
Having the most holy image of the Lord
and that of the most pure Mother of God,
the great and saintly man presented the small infant,
                                     Uglješa Despotović.

His innocent early age entered eternity;
And his body, created in sin by his ancestors,
Was buried in the Grave.

Bend down, O Christ, the Lord,
And you, most pure Mother of God,
To me--miserable.
Take care of the passing away of my soul,
Which I saw in those who have born me
And in the infant whom I have born.
The sorrow for him is burning steadily in my heart
And I am overcome by my motherly ways.

And let the immaculate Mother of God of Hilandar
Be his judge on the day of the terrible Judgement.
Amen.

Source:

This poem was written on the backside of a folding icon
    as gold-inlaid silver tablets. It is located on
    Mount Athos in the Monastery Hilandar.

The Encomium to Prince Lazar[1]

Since your youth, you have been brought up in the beautiful things of this world. As a new martyr, Prince Lazar, the strong hand of the Lord showed you as strong and famous among all rulers on the earth. You ruled your fatherland; and, in all good things, you cheered the Christians under your protection. With a manly heart, and with a desire for piousness, you faced the serpent and the enemy of God's churches, having judged that it would have been unbearable for your heart to see the Christians of your fatherland overwhelmed by the Moslems; if you could not accomplish this, you would leave the glory of your kingdom on earth to perish, and having become purple with your own blood, you would join the soldiers of the heavenly kingdom. In this way, your two wishes were fulfilled. You killed the serpent, and you received from God the wreath of martyrdom. Do not forget, now, your beloved children, whom you left as orphans with your passing away. Since you have been true in heavenly eternal bliss, many sorrows and affliations have come upon your beloved children. They are living in much sorrow; and, conquered by the Moslems, they are in need of your help. Therefore, I am begging you, pray to our Lord Almighty for your beloved children and for all those who are serving them with love and faith, for your beloved children are burdened with much grief. Those who were eating your children's bread rose up in mutiny, and they made the people forget your good deeds, oh martyr. Although you have passed away from this life, you know the sorrows and the afflictions of your children; and, like a martyr having courage before God, bend your knees before the Lord, who bestowed upon you the crown of martyrdom and ask him to grant your beloved children long life in peace and God's favor. Pray that the Orthodox Christians keep to their faith without fail in your absence; ask God, the victor, to award victory to your beloved children, Prince Stefan and Vuk,[3] against invisible and visible enemies. When you receive help from God, we will offer you praise and thankfulness. Gather the assembly of your interlocutors, the holy martyrs; and, with them all, pray to God, who honored you. Let George know, call on Demetrius, convince Theodor, bring with you Merkurij and Prokopij, and do not forget the forty Sebastian Martyrs. Your beloved children, Prince Stefan and Vuk,[4] are fighting in their martyrdom. Pray to God to help them; come to our aid wherever you are. Look at my small gifts and consider them large. I did not offer you praise according to your dignity, but according to the power of my limited mind; hence I am expecting a small reward; but you were not paltry; my dear master and holy martyr in this perishable and fleeting life, and much less so now in the eternal and great life which you have received from God. You have

nourished me plentifully although I was a stranger among
strangers. Now I am asking of you two things: nourish
me and soften the fierce storm of my soul and body.
Jefimija is presenting this to you eagerly, oh Saint.

NOTES

[1] Prince Lazar Hrebeljanović (1371-1389), descended from the Nemanjić dynasty through the female line.
[2] A probable reference to Murad, the Turkish Sultan, who died in the battle of Kosovo.
[3] Vukan.
[4] Vukan.

Sources:

Jefimija, despot Uglješa widow, wove a burial shroud in
    golden and silver thread in honor of the Serbian
    Tzar Lazar. It is now located in the monastery of
    Vrdnik (Ravanica), in Srem (Yugoslavia).

Prayer to Lord Jesus Christ

Out of a sinful mouth,
From an odious heart
And polluted tongue,
From my sinful soul, accept the prayer,
Oh my Christ;[1]
And neither turn me away, your servant,
Nor accuse me with your fury, Oh Lord,
At the moment of my departure.
And do not punish[2] me with your anger
On the day of Your coming,
Since before your judgment, Oh Lord,[4]
I have been already judged by my conscience;
Not a single hope of salvation is there in me,
Unless your mercy conquers the multitude of my
    transgressions.
For this reason, I pray to You, Oh kind Lord,
Do not turn aside this small gift,
Which I am presenting to the holy Temple of your
    venerable Mother
And my hope, the Virgin Mary of Hilandar;
As I accepted the widow's faith
Who brought you two coins, Lord,[5]

So, in the same way, I brought this, your unworthy
    servant, Jefimija, the nun, Oh, Mistress,
The daughter of the ruler Vojihna, my master,
Who is buried here and who was once a despot.
This curtain was contributed,
To the temple of the Holy Virgin of Hilandar
In the year 6907, indiction[6]
And if someone were to remove this gift
From the temple of the Holy Virgin of Hilandar,
Let him be separated from her One and Indivisible
    Trinity.

NOTES

[1] Words from a communion prayer by the Byzantine mystic Simeon, The Theologian.

[2-4] These words were written under the influence of the communion prayer by Simeon Metaphrast (second part of the 10th century).

[5] This passage was inspired by the Biblical passage (Mark 12, 41-44) which described a widow who donated all her possessions, consisting of two coins, to God's treasury.

[6] 6907 from the creation of the world. According to this reckoning, from the creation of the world until Christ's birth 5508 years elapsed. After deducting this number from the year of world's creation, years of the area will be obtained (A.D.). An indiction consists of 15 years.

Sources:

Jefimija embroidered this prayer with golden and silver
    thread in many colors. The embroidery was intended
    for the main alter door in the Monastery Hilandar
    on Mount Athos, where her son, Uglješa, and her
    father, Vojihna, were buried. The embroidery is
    now located in Hilandar.

ARCHBISHOP DANILO
c. 1270 - 1337

There are several medieval Serbian authors with the name Danilo. This author is known as Danilo II; he was an Archbishop of the Serbian Orthodox Church during 1323-1337. He wrote biographies of Serbian medieval rulers, including the biography of Jelena, the wife of King Stefan Dragutin. His monumental work is referred to in the poetry of Serbian folklore as "knjige starostavne" and "knjige carostavne"--"the ancients books" and "the royal books." As a result of his work, many historical details concerning both the rulers of medieval Serbia and the members of the Nemanjić dynasty have been preserved.

The Lives of Serbian Kings and Archbishops: Queen Jelena's[1] Death

While in her royal headquarters in the place called Brnjaci, this blessed lady, Jelena, became more ill and realized that the day of her passing had arrived. She selected many honorable monks and old priests to be with her at that moment. When they arrived, Jelena, with weary face and sorrowful eyes, opened her sweet-speaking mouth and said: "'...Brethren, fathers, and my beloved children, know that my life is nearing its end and that my soul is very sorrowful before my death....'[2] and I am certain that I will not escape from death with this sickness." When they heard these blessed words, there was much grief, sobbing, and cries of sorrow. They spoke with bitter tears: "Oh, good lady and our mother, why do you make our souls grieve so unexpectedly? As we listen to these words of yours, we are perplexed and shaken by untimely grief." This blessed lady consoled them in a most dignified way with the sweet words flowing from her mouth; and in that moment, without hesitation, she started sending messengers to all parts of her country--to bishops, abbots, and all the other important persons--saying in her message, "Come, oh my beloved ones, and see my passing away. I am leaving on a journey on which I have never gone before." All of them heard these words from their lady and gentle protectress, and, I tell you, my beloved ones, it was similar to the time when the Mother of God passed away, and the apostles, seized by clouds, went to her burial. Such was the passing away of this blessed lady. It seemed to me, the sinner, that the Holy Spirit called people everywhere to hurry to the passing away of this blessed one, so fast did all the regions of the country hear about this Christ-loving lady. Verily, I saw people coming from all sides--distinguished ones as well as poor ones, travelers, lame, and blind ones--all whose protectress was this blessed lady of mine. All of the Serbian regions, gathered at her famous palace Brnjaci; and I, humble Danilo, being at that time bishop of the Church of the Holy Apostle of Christ and First Martyr, Archdeacon Stefan, in Banjska, as soon as I heard about the imminent passing of the blessed lady, hastened forth as fast as my strength allowed and found myself there with other brethren, bishops, heads of monasteries, abbots, and the whole congregation of her country. And when the blessed lady Jelena heard about our arrival, and, moreover, when she saw us, she lifted herself from the deathbed she was lying on, and, raising her hands to heavenly heights, she said, "I thank You, my Lord and my master, Jesus Christ, generous and merciful lover of men, that You deigned to grant me, Your sinful servant, today, on the last day of my life, to see with my eyes the arrival of my lords, Your servants and helpers, and to hear their words and their heavenly singing so that I might rejoice in Your sweetest name." After that she said, "Saintly fathers begin singing to God whatever customary church hymns you know." All of us, who stood around her blessed deathbed and watched her, could see that her face was like the face of God's angel or like dawn, shining with beautiful rays of many bright colors. As we realized that she was about to pass away, seized with grief, we cried out, sobbing, "Oh, our lady and mother, we see you quite ready to depart." We then started singing funeral songs and did everything else appropriate for the passing away of this blessed one. With us, there was the God-loving man, the most holy bishop from Raška, Master Pavle. After a little while, she received the holy and sublime sacrament; and having composed a prayer, she prayed to God for the entire state of her fatherland, saying with tears in her eyes, "I thank You, oh my sweet Jesus, for all of the favors that You did not deny me, a sinner, from the first day of my life until now. I pray to You, oh God; look down with Your merciful eyes from Your glorious throne on the state of my fatherland, which You presented to me. Strengthen it with Your

almighty right hand and bestow on Your people the fear of
Your holy name. Fortify Your servants and my sons in
Your love so that they will praise You properly with a
pure heart every day of their lives. And I pray to You
for the whole world, oh Lord; let it have, as Your gift,
a quiet and peaceful life, and preserve with Your
strength all those who pay homage on the day of my
death." She bid peace to the whole congregation which
stood before the face of this blessed one, saying, "Peace
to you, oh masters, fathers and brothers, and assembly of
priests; peace to you honorable monks; peace to you
priests and all the church assembly; peace to you, too,
my beloved children; and peace to you, the poor, humble,
and weak ones, for you prayed to God for me, a sinner,
and you were heard." Having bestowed a blessing on all,
from the humble to the proud, and having strengthened
each one separately with the sweet words of her admoni-
tion, she made the sign of the cross with her hand and
said: "...into thy hand I commend my spirit...."[3] So,
praising God's glory, she gave up her spirit; and after
that there were loud cries and sobbing in all the regions of the blessed lady's state, and the most holy
bishops, then desiring to lay to rest the body of the
blessed lady Jelena, took it and by walking humbly and
singing funeral hymns, the congregation began to carry
the body to its grave. There was at the time of her
passing a turbulent wind, and a fierce winter was upon
the land. Because of this, we proceeded slowly with the
body of the blessed one. Several times after walking
small distances, we would rest and sing many laudable
holy hymns. Finally, carrying the body of the blessed
one, we arrived with splendid glory at her famous monastery, Gradac.[4] Here, having made all the usual ar-
rangements with the most holy monks of that place about
the burial of the blessed one, we did not want to bury
her body until the arrival of her son, the beloved,
pious, supreme King Stefan Uroš. After waiting awhile,
there arrived the most holy archbishop, Master Sava, and,
after him, the whole assembly of the great church.
After that came the pious king, the son of the blessed
one, with all the nobles and all the powerful men in
their imperial glory. The king started crying and sobbing very much, pulling hairs from his head, flinging
himself forward above his God-loving mother's body,
striking his face and sobbing, "Oh, my mother and my
lady, how will I, unworthy one, forget the longings of

your heart and the sorrow your mind suffered for me? Christ breathed spirit into me, and you brought me up, instructing me with your wise words of advice from the inexhaustible spring of your honey-flowing mouth. But, oh my gentle sustainer and strong and impregnable fortress of your fatherland, my heart is full of much sobbing and crying, and I am undecided which devout song my lips should express in your praise, oh blessed one, but because of my limited mind, I can only cry out praising your greatness and say, "Blessed are you, my mother, royal lady, the sweetest sustainer of my youth and the defender of my life; blessed are you, because of your effort and your devout deeds, this dwelling was built to the holy Trinity; blessed are you, since surrounding yourself with a sign of the cross, you have torn the devil's snares; blessed are you, my mother and my lady, for you have sown the seed of Christ's good fruit into the furrows of your soul; blessed are you, as you washed with the spring of your tears the filth of body and soul; blessed are you for your unutterable merciful deeds to the poor and the strangers, which made God appear merciful to you; blessed are you, for you fed the poor and consoled the sad and found justice for the injured; blessed are you, for you protected us in battles with prayers pleasing to God; blessed are you, as the children of your fatherland rejoice in praising you; blessed are you, for your name has been inscribed in the books of lives; blessed are you, for you joined the congregation of long-suffering martyred women; blessed are you, my lady and my mother, inexhaustible source of live water, sustaining the youth of the famous child of your fatherland; blessed are you, since your prayers strengthened the state sceptre of pious kings of the whole Serbian land; blessed is the soil which receives the salve of your body and blessed is the holy temple which receives your blessed body; blessed are you, my lady and my mother, and let me repeat, blessed; with the help of your sinful prayers, I hope to receive forgiveness for my sins on the terrible day of judgment of all men." When her beloved son, the noble and supreme King Uroš ended these laudable words, all those present, the humble and the proud, burst into thunderous crying and sobbing which lasted for a long time. It was if the ground itself were rising and the insensitive stone was transforming itself, responding to the cries and sobs at the sight of the king crying bitterly and overwhelmed with a flood of tears. After all the preparations for the burial had been made, the noble and supreme King Stefan Uroš took with his hands the body of his mother, the blessed lady Jelena, and accompanied by the most holy archbishop, Master Sava, and with the assembly of venerable bishops and abbots singing psalms and other devout songs, carried the body to the grave which was already prepared. They were followed by the consecrated assembly and the king's council of elders and other noblemen and landlords of that Christ-loving lady, and by all the people of her fatherland. They placed Jelena in the grave prepared for her in the great and magnificent church of the most holy Virgin Mother of God which, in honor of her good tidings, was built by the blessed lady Jelena herself from its foundations as befitting its name. Also, the noble and Christ-loving King Stefan Uroš gave away many alms on that day to all the poor, the strangers, and the weak who happened to be there during his blessed lady mother's passing away. Having made a feast with the whole congregation of his fatherland and having refreshed himself in body and soul, he again returned to his royal throne. The others dispersed, each in his own way glorifying Holy Trinity, Father, Son, and the Holy Spirit, and praising the memory of Christ's servant, the very venerable Jelena.

NOTES

[1] Helen of Anjou was married to the Serbian King Stefan Uroš I (1243-1276). She is the mother of two Serbian kings, Stefan Dragutin and Stefan Uroš II, Milutin. This is the first Serbian biography of a woman.

[2] Matthew 26:38, Mark 14:34.

[3] Luke 23:46.

[4] Not far from the town of Raška. It is the only monastery built in a Gothic architectural style in Medieval Serbia.

Sources:

The question of whether this manuscript was written by archbishop Danilo II or his disciples has not yet been resolved. It exists in three versions: (1) the Russo-Slavonic version from Sremski Karlovci (now the Library of the Patriarchate in Belgrade) dating to 1763, (2) another Russo-Slavonic version from 1780 and (3) a Serbo-Slavonic version from the 16th century, taken from the University Library of Lwow (USSR). Djura Daničić edited *The Lives of Serbian Kings and Archbishops* in Zagreb in 1866 by transcribing the Russo-Slavonic text, which he considered more accurate, into Serbo-Slavonic. The same book appeared as a reprint in *Životi Kraljeva i Archiepiskopa Srpskih*, Variorum Reprints, London, 1972.

"The Life of St. Milutin"

My honorable and Christ-loving master, the most august, mighty, and autocratic King Stefan Uroš, was the son of glorious parents, the great Serbian King Uroš and the Christ-loving Jelena, who was his mother. Furthermore, this young man was a favorite of God from his very youth, marked by the spirit of grace of the power of the Lord. This child was begotten by wisdom, nursed by grace, and raised by the Holy Spirit. The very right hand of the Lord's might crowned his head with an unwithering crown and He presented him to his country as a truly luminous light, who progressed by God's providence, to distinguish himself by God-pleasing deeds and to rule these parts of his native country which had been squandered. He was a good shepherd of the reason-endowed sheep of this entire territory, their good teacher and instructor, a relentless builder of churches of God, and not only a builder [of new ones], but also a re-builder of those that were laid in ruins, in order to bring everyone to the true faith. Because of this and because of his extraordinary physical beauty and handsome features, his name became famous among all the nations and empires, so that many emperors who were his neighbours, hearing of his benevolent attitude, sought his friendship. Let our mind not be perplexed on account of this blessed one when we hear that emperors with such majestic names loved him so, that they honored him with their august affection and multiplied his immense royal wealth, and that many mighty ones were his subordinates, for the almighty God and Lord, the Emperor of the Universe, was fond of him; that is why they, too, were fond of him.

However, having said this much, we shall interrupt this narration and we shall now attempt to depict the temptations of this honorable and Christ-loving [man], the multitude of tribulations he had to endure in his youth from many foreign emperors; all that, God willing, we shall include in his writing; how God saved him from them, and how, by His help, he withstood them all and defeated their malice, majestically destroying their vainglorious pride.

* * * * *

After the honorable King Uroš defeated all his malicious enemies and after God had firmly strengthened his throne, and when his entire country enjoyed a calm and peaceful life, this Christ-loving [man] who truly loved [his] children, wanted his beloved son, whose name was Stefan, to marry, and he took the daughter of the Bulgarian emperor Smiljac and betrothed her to him as his wife. He gave him a considerable part of his own state, the country of Zeta with all its cities and provinces. He bestowed upon him all the honors of imperial rank and having given to him all he needed, both small as well as great, he bade him leave to go to that country which he himself had set aside for him. And after [his son] had lived a long time in the state of that country together with his noblemen, the latter, overpowered by the Devil's manipulation, maliciously plotted together and, at an opportune moment, came to this honorable and beloved son of the honorable King Uroš and, with flattering words, diverted him from his father's love, saying to him, "It is proper for you to take the throne of your father and we will all help you so that your will may be done in everything. If you do not comply with our demand we shall no longer consider ourselves subject to you." And having spoken to him with such deceitful words for a long time, they achieved what they wanted. And from that time, this beloved son of his inclined his heart toward such deceptive words and refused to listen to the words of his father who had raised him in true faith and chastity, in love and wisdom. And he [the son] began to entertain the ambition to take away his [father's] throne; and when there was a great feud between them, he [the son] began to lure the noblemen of his most exhalted king with deceitful words [asking them] to abandon their master and come over to him. Many of them, yielding to temptation, defected from this honorable king to his son.

And the honorable King Uroš, seeing the actions of his son, began to advise him with humble and sweet words to come to him. However, he [the son] did not pay heed to these words but instead committed even worse offences against his father. And my master, having seen his [son's] irreconcilable intention, gathered his soldiers and went with them to his son's state, the country of Zeta. And he [the son], having seen the arrival of his father, fled across the river known as Bojana. And then, this most exhalted king sent him this message with its God-inspired words which should have induced him to accept his [father's] authority, saying, "My dear and beloved child, I call you and you do not answer me. In my affliction, it appears that you are near me, but [when] I stretch out my hand I do not find you. Many tears blind me and a stinging pain rends my heart because of your separation; I am overwhelmed by the flames of many sighs. My child, this I did not expect from you. Come, my dear son, that I, an old man, might be consoled." And with many such words he persuaded him to return; and at the beginning, he [the son] had a long conversation with his father from across the river, and after that he fell on his knees before him [the father] and said, "I sinned against you, Father." However, contemplating, he [the father] thought to himself: "I realize that I have reached quite an old age and I anticipate that in the future I should expect many afflictions and sorrows from this son of mine, if I let him go free." And he took council with many of his noblemen concerning this one so dear to him, and they told him, "Honorable King, what you intend [to do] is reasonable." Thus, at that moment, he ordered his son to be seized, put in fetters and that his body be wrapped in iron chains; and they took him to the famous city of Skopje. And after he had stayed for some time in that city, this honorable king sent some of his confidants who took him [the son] and blinded him.

Sources:

Church Slavonic Text published in ŽK.
Serbo-Croatian translation published in: KFD; SSK, II.
*Život kraljeva i arhiepiskopa srpskih od Arhiepiskopa
    Danila II.* Lazar Mirković, tr. Beograd: Srpska
    književna zadruga. 1935.

The Lament Over Dragutin
[An Excerpt from "The Life of Dragutin"]

Why did you leave us,
our gentle shepherd and teacher?
Who shall replace you,
who can be your equal
in defending your native country?
Your name was feared by all malefactors!
Through the help of your Lord Christ,
you found the lost
and gathered the dispersed,
and enriched the poor,
and raised the fallen
and exhalted the humble;
you manifested the simple and unknown as wonderful
and florious in your native country.
One cannot enumerate all your good deeds,
O blessed one,
for which God glorified you forever.
Because, with the spiritual sickle,
you have cut down to the roots
the heretical week,
thereby becoming
the abode of the Holy Spirit.

Sources:

Church Slavonic text published in ŽK.
Serbo-Croatian text published in SSK, II.
*Životi kraljeva i arhiepiskopa arpskih od Archiepiskopa
    Danila II*. Lazar Mirković, tr. Beograd: Srpska
    književna zadruga. Beograd. 1935.

MILICA HREBELJANOVIC (JEVGENIJA)
(c. 1353 - 1405)

Jevgenija's secular name was Milica. She was the daughter of Prince Vratko and wife of Prince Lazar (d.+1389). After the execution of her husband, ordered by Bayazid, Milica ruled for some time in Serbia until her son, Stefan Lazarević, was old enough to take the throne. At that time, much wisdom and personal courage was needed to reign in a country which was nominally free yet actually invaded by the Turks. It was difficult to maintain a national spirit without provoking the Turks and without giving them an excuse to kill and plunder. Milica proved herself an able ruler of the country at a very trying period. Her personal tragedy (losing her husband and sending her daughter Mara to the harem of Bayazid, who had ordered the execution of her husband Lazar in 1389) did not interfere with her carrying out her duties.

It appears that her grief and loneliness were captured in her highly lyrical and poetic address to Prince Lazar. Although conceived as a church hymn, it contains a personal note and lyrical tones unusual for solemn and somber church hymnody.

Mother's Prayer

O God, who as the Holy Trinity
has been hymned with awe
by bodiless powers [angels]
before all ages,
and who, from the time of the incarnation
of Thy Only-begotten and Inseparable Son,
our Lord Jesus Christ,
through the All-pure and All-holy
Virgin Mother of God,
accept also praises and spiritual services
from us sinners;
O Master,
the Inscrutable Wisdom of the Father,
look mercifully upon my sins,
strengthen my children in the true faith
and in serene ways,
so that they may virtuously serve Thee,
their God,

as did their Master and Father
the Prince [lazar] of the blessed memory.

Sources:

[Excerpt from an Edict to Monastery Dečani issued by
    Milica and her sons Stefan and Vuk in 1397.]
Church Slavonic text published in: Miklošić, Franjo.
    Monumenta Serbica. Viennae. 1858.

Who Is This One?

Who is this one?
Whisper into my ears!
Is this the one for whom I used to long,
my jewel, the gatherer of my dispersed children?
Is this the one whom enemies wanted to destroy out of
    envy,
the light of my sight whom they wanted to incarcerate
and keep in the dark dungeon,
but could not?
Is this the bridegroom of my widowhood?

Come, O bridegroom,
Come and repay those who do evil to me
according to their deeds,
for they failed to understand
that you would come to my aid.
Take up arms and rise and do not tarry,
plunge into their hearts the sharp arrows
which they, the evil ones,
have sharpened against me.
I cannot stand their mockery.
Oh, with how many odious offences they plagued me.
Come, avenge me with your blood.
Come, O my helper, at the time of my falling.
Gather my dispersed children
who have been taken from me
by the envy of my enemies.
Gather them within my fence;
and guard my children
so that the wolf does not feed himself upon my flock
nor disperse them with his envy,
as he had done before when you were not with them.
Let your eyes not sleep,
let your feet not become weak,

guard my flock which I entrust to you.
Chase the barbarian infidels away from them.
Do not cease to fight them,
[defending] me and my flock.

Rejoice, O Lazar,
my never-sleeping eye.
And, to repeat what was already said at the beginning:
Lazar is the one who by his radiance
excels the brightness of the stars;
Lazar is the victim of invaders,
the confessor of the Trinity,
the liberator of the captives;
Lazar is the strong pillar of the Church,
a doctor to the sick, raiment to the naked;
Lazar is the mighty leader
and saviour of the monks,
and a firm [adversary] of demons.
Rejoice, O Lazar,
I hymn you in the manner of apostles
and I repeat: Rejoice,
rejoice, O lily which sprang from a thorn,
O invincible weapon of soldiers;
rejoice, O teacher of hermits;
rejoice, O Lazar,
the rudder and the calm haven of seafarers.
Rejoice, O avenger of the wronged
and the reprimander of liars.
Rejoice, O comforter of mourners
and defender of the poor and raiment of the naked.
Rejoice, O beauty of the strong ones
and the protector of widows.
Blessed are you, indeed, Lazar;
bless me, the one who blesses you.
There is no praise of which you would not be worthy,
but my wit is getting tired...

Sources:

Serbo-Croatian translation published in: *Staro srpsko
    pesništvo:* X-XVIII veka. Bagdala, 1966.

The Office for Prince Martyr Lazar

Several authors, rather than one, are credited with the the authorship of the entire text of this *Office for Prince Martyr Lazar*. "Canon to Prince Martyr Lazar" is ascribed to an anonymous monk of the Monastery Ravanica, "Hymn to Prince Martyr Lazar" to a different monk of the same monastery, "Milica's Lament" to still another monk from that monastery, and the "Narration about the Prince Martyr Lazar" to Danilo III. Some literary historians believe that Grigorije Camblak and/or Jelena Mrnjavčević [Jefimija] could also have been authors of some portions of this *Office for Prince Martyr Lazar*. The translated portions included in this anthology are from the *Office for Prince Martyr Lazar* and *Office Commemorating the Transfer of Prince Martyr Lazar's Relics*.

Anonymous Monk of the Monastery Ravanica

CANNON TO PRINCE MARTYR LAZAR [With Acrostic]
Original acrostic: LAZARA POHVALITI, BOŽE MOJ, RAZUM DARUJ MI. Acrostic in English: SEND ME WISDOM, O' MY LORD, TO PRAISE LAZARUS.

Standing near the throne of God,
    shining with resplendent radiance,
    rejoicing incessantly with the angels,
    pray that my tenebrous soul may be enlightened
    in order that I may hymn properly
    your memory, O Lazarus.

Even though we, your commemorators,
    may not be able to praise you fittingly;
    nevertheless, according to our ability,
    we are weaving a new hymn
    honoring your glorious memory,
    telling of your life and martyrdom.
    Being a loving father,
    accept this praise,
    disregarding its weakness.

No later than from your very youth,
    you adopted the fear of God
    as the font of your virtuous life,
    O Lazarus.
    It guided you toward the right path

and, having walked along it,
You entered into the mansions of the Lord.

Definitely knowing
    that you are placed above the angels,
    O Virgin ever-praised,
    we, the faithful people
    of your Son and God,
    glorify you
    and pray from the bottom of our souls:
    deliver us who are praising you
    from the invasion of enemies.

Marvelous wisdom and divine grace
    were bestowed upon you
    in your infancy;
    and you were rich in all kinds of virtues.
    You distributed your wealth to the poor;
    and for this, Christ enriched you
    with great wealth in heaven.

Equal to Abraham you were
    by your hospitality in this life.
    Your right hand was very generous
    to strangers and the sick,
    and to travellers
    it offered hospitality;
    thereby you also became worthy
    of receiving God Himself.

With the beauty of good deeds,
    you have adorned
    your rich and famous home on earth,
    O Lazarus of the blessed memory,
    in order to receive the reward from above,
    O wise one;
    From there you have received
    the right to the Kingdom of Heaven.

Immaculate and most truly, Virgin,
    having your prayers
    as armor and protection,
    the brave warrior of your Son and God
    defeated the leader of the Turks,
    and for himself he earned
    the glory of martyrs.

Similar to the sanctuary of God
    you became through your merits,
    for you have built
    a magnificent church for Him,
    which amazed everyone
    by its abundance;
    and there you settled
    a multitude of monks.

Distinguished Lazarus,
    the talent of power,
    which was deservingly awarded to you,
    you did not bury in the earth,
    as the lazy servant did;
    but, having worked with it
    as a vigilant servant of your Lord,
    you returned it, multiplied, to Him.

Of the God-pleasing life of Job of Uz,
    your virtuous life reminds us;
    you excelled in knowledge and wisdom.
    Adorned with modesty
    and shining with the nobility of your life,
    you later received,
    O Lazarus,
    even more precious gifts.

Mother of God,
    singing praises to you,
    we, your faithful people,
    falling on our knees,
    pray to you, the Pure One:
    O Lady, pray with the holy martyrs
    for those who honor you;
    for everything is possible to you
    who has been blessed by God
    and who Has given birth to Christ.

Of the virtuous Joseph,
    you remind us
    by the purity and piety of your life;
    you were a generous donor of wheat to the poor
    and, having planted it thereby
    in the furrows drained by poverty
    at the time of harvest,
    you reaped the sheaves of joy.

Mercy you earned
>	by your own generosity
>	during your lifetime.
>	As a recompense for your righteousness,
>	an inexhaustible prize was in store for you;
>	now that you have received it
>	as a reward for your endeavours,
>	you abide in joy
>	with the hosts of martyrs and the righteous.

Yea, noble Lazarus,
>	those who are bitterly oppressed by poverty,
>	and those who are in captivity,
>	and all those plagued by all kinds of tribulations
>	solemnly proclaim here, in the subsolar region,
>	the ineffable vastness of your generosity.

Lo, Mother of God,
>	you gave birth
>	to the Divine Word of God
>	immaculately,
>	without knowing marriage,
>	in accordance with His will.
>	For this same God,
>	whom he confessed,
>	the glorious martyr Lazarus
>	accepted death,
>	courageously and voluntarily.

O holy one,
>	how beautiful is your purchase,
>	how wonderful your trade:
>	with transitory and insignificant glory
>	you have purchased the eternal one.
>	Enjoying it now,
>	pray for us.

Really, Lazarus,
>	who would not admire your life:
>	As a wise bee, you have collected
>	a multitude of flower-like virtues;
>	and, adorned with them,
>	you bestow a pleasant aroma upon us.

Deservingly, you have earned from Christ
>	the glory you longed for

by your God-pleasing life.
Now that you are enjoying it,
clad in the resplendent attire of good deeds,
rejoice!

True and never-changing Virgin Mother,
the Immaculate Word
became fond of you
because of your chastity.
After He was born of you,
He regenerated all men.
He is the One
Who glorified through miracles
the one who pleased Him.

Owing to your sincere faith in God,
you have rebuilt many holy churches,
and erected even more new ones
for the glory of God.
Because of this,
you have made yourself
an abode of the Holy Spirit.

Precisely, as a talented architect,
you have built a beautiful ladder
here on earth
which reaches heaven;
your good deeds served as the steps for it,
and by climbing upon them,
you have reached
what you have longed for,
exclaiming:
"Blessed is the God of our fathers!"

Rather early,
even before your martyrdom,
you, the wise one,
were endowed with wisdom
and a virtuous life.
After your wonderful sacrifice,
you became even more beautiful.
We, therefore, honor you
as one of God's favorites,
and we proclaim:
"Blessed is the God of our fathers!"

Adam was redeemed from corruption
   by the One
   Whom you have born immaculately,
   O Virgin.
   Save me, too,
   from rotting in evil,
   for the sake of the prayers
   which your Lazarus
   offers to God.

Immersed in and adorned with a radiance
   similar to the light of the sun,
   O Lazarus,
   vested in the royal purple
   which was colored
   by the redness of your blood,
   holding the cross in your hands,
   you stand in front of Christ,
   Who has glorified you.
   We, therefore, supplicate you:
   entreat Him that we may receive eternal life
   on account of your martyrdom.

Songs of praise and prayers of your people
   should reach you;
   and because of your love for your country,
   look upon the plight of your flock,
   and combat those
   who war ferociously against us;
   for we know how powerful
   is the prayer of the righteous.

Even though our prayers may be brief
   and deprived of beauty,
   do not reject them,
   we beseech you, O Lazarus,
   dweller in the Heavenly Kingdom,
   but look upon your flock,
   now that you are departed,
   as you have done
   during your lifetime,
   and provide peace for our Despot
   and for us who honor you.

Listen, O pious people: enjoy,
   for a bright star

appeared in the west most recently,
shining with the wonderful rays
of its virtues
and enlightening the faithful.
Lazarus, wealthy in blessings!
Feast, therefore, and proclaim:
"Bless the Lord, all His creatures!"

An angelic greeting
we offer to you, O God's Bride:
rejoice, O Helper of the people
who truthfully honor you,
O Fulfillment of prophets' prophecies,
O divinely beautiful Adornment
of apostles and martyrs.

Zealously, the church of the faithful,
having assembled today
at the festive anniversary of your death,
celebrates with all its neighbours
the acquisition of a brave guardian
and defender who shelters her
with his protection;
let us praise him!

After you have adorned your soul
with divine beauties,
you stepped in glory
before the Beautiful Word,
fearing nothing.
We, therefore, entreat you:
look mercifully from above
upon us who sing to you.
Grant to our Despot
victory over his enemies,
and we shall bless you.

Rejoice, O hosts of commemorators
gathered at the celebration
of the already glorified Lazarus;
let us enjoy this redeeming celebration,
for we have seen today
the fulfillment of the prophecy
saying that the righteous
shall live forever,
and that their glory

is bestowed upon them
   by the same God
   Whom we glorify.

Unbelievably previous and unexpendable wealth
   is your body,
   in which a temple abides.
   After being adorned by you,
   it proclaims:
   "My glory glorifies God
   Who has given me this adornment,
   a shelter and protection
   from my enemies."

Seeing in you
   the true Mother of God,
   the martyr Lazarus,
   proclaiming faith in the One
   Who was born of you,
   and strengthened by His love,
   confronted courageously
   a multitude of the godless
   and fought them
   until his death.
   O Mother of God,
   we praise you.

Hymn to Prince-Martyr Lazar

Who would not glorify you,
a zealous follower of God's commandments,
or who would not praise
your wonderful life?
Like an industrious bee,
you have collected
manifold virtues,
trying to exchange
mundane glory
for the future one.
You were the eye of the blind,
the leg of the maimed,
a staff to the elderly;
you were all to all
by your generous hand.
You adorned your head
with the crown of martyrdom;

you stand in Christ's presence,
enjoying His glory.
Pray to Him,
we beseech you, O wise Lazar,
that you may rest forever in peace, earned by your deeds,
and that our souls may be saved.

"Milica's Lament"

[Depicts Stefan and Vuk, the sons of Prince Lazar, walking in front of Lazar's coffin and lamenting:]

"Woe to us, our lord and father,
many sorrows and tribulations have befallen us
from the time you had left us."

This and many other things they spoke weeping. And as their mother [Princess Milica] saw this, she fell as if dead over that saintly body and for a long time she was unconscious. Later [having come to herself], as if awakened from a deep sleep, she scratched her face and pulled out her hair as she said:

"Woe to me, O my light,
how were you eclipsed from my sight,
how did [you] my beauty become so darkened,
how did [you] wilt, my sweet flower,
how did you go past us through your martyrdom?
Where is your sweetly-speaking tongue,
where is your honey-pouring mouth,
Oh, mountains, hills, and forest trees,
cry with me today.
Henceforth my eyes pour
bloody streams of tears."

This and much more she spoke wailing.
All the people witnessed this, beating their
chests, and their mourning augmented the weeping.
And holding candles and censers, they accompanied
the saintly remnants. And I, myself, saw all
this happen.

Sources:

Church Slavonic text (manuscript): *MHM*, #482; #509.
Portions of Church Slavonic text published in: Ćorović,

"Siluan i Danilo II," *Glas Srpske Kraljevske Akademije*, CXXXVI, drugi razred, 72. Sremski Karlovci. 1928.

Glasnik društva srpske slovesnosti, knj. XI. Beograd. 1859.

Glasnik Srpskog Učenog Drustva, XXI. Beograd. 1867.

Srpski književni glasnik, knj. XII, br. 5. Beograd. 1925

Church Slavonic text and Serbo-Croatian translation (portions) published in: Trifunović, Djordje, Dimitrije Bogdanović, et al. *Srbljak*, 4 volumes. Beograd. 1970.

Serbo-Croatian translation only (portions) published in *ISSK; KFD; SSK*, III.

DANILO III
c. 1350--between 1396-1399

    Danilo III was a high official of the Serbian Orthodox Church. In 1382, he was the abbot of the Monastery Drenča, and from 1390, the Patriarch of the Serbian Orthodox Church. As an author, he distinguished himself by including in his works concrete details, dramatic scenes, and dialogues.
    Danilo III is the author of *The Office for St. Sava, The Office for St. Simeon, The Office for St. Milutin*, and, probably, the "Narration about Prince Lazar." There are, however, literary historians who question Danilo's authorship of the "Narration" and ascribe it to some anonymous monk from the Monastery Ravanica. The "Narration" was written shortly after the Battle of Kosovo, which took place in 1389; and it represents a report of an eye-witness, or at least a contemporary. It includes many details concerning the situation in Raška before the Battle of Kosovo. It was written in 1392-93, and, most likely, by Danilo III.
    The Office for St. Milutin is written in the tradition of Orthodox hymnography and it clearly attests to Danilo's poetic talent.

"A Narration about Prince Lazar"

"To the descendants in memory of the holy and blessed Prince Lazar, formerly the sovereign of the entire Serbian Country."

    The holy and forever remembered Prince Lazar was of Serbian ancestry, by fatherland, birth, and upbringing. He was of glorious, illustrious, and distinguished forefathers and was born of pious parents. Nourished by the Holy Spirit, after his birth, he grew up and excelled among the great ones. Upon reaching adulthood, he was given to the service of Tzar Dušan,[1] who was ruling then; and because of his modesty, good nature, virtue, and courage, the Tzar distinguished him with the honor of being the first in his palace. By the order of the sovereign, he took as his wife a Tzar's relative, the daughter of a nobleman. She was also of an illustrious, glorious, and distinguished family of sovereign origin, descended from the clan of holy Simeon Nemanja,[2] the first ruler of the Serbs. Lazar was the father of many sons and daughters.

Finally, after many years, Tzar Stefan left his transitory life for infinite eternity, and his successor to the Tzardom was Tzar Uroš,[3] his son. So, they held and directed the Serbian sceptre. After a short time, Tzar Uroš died from much sorrow and misfortune caused by his own people. Then, by providence and the grace of God, and because of his modesty, honesty, piety, and good nature, this forever remembered man, Prince Lazar, was elevated to the Serbian throne. He was blessed by the archbishop's hands first, and then by the congregation of the entire Serbian clergy and council, and so he became the Serbian sovereign. He spent his life in pursuring different acts of virtue, modesty, and good deeds. He was very modest, mild, generous, and fair, like few other men. He was not like a ruler, but like a father with his children, instructing and directing them. Archbishops, priests, and monks were paid homage; old men were respected according to the Epistles; noblemen were met; the young were instructed and were given love. He defended those who were victims of injustice. His eyes showed compassion, and his hand was outstretched and ready to give. Those who did not have any clothes were warmly clad; strangers were housed; the weak were comforted; and the faraway monasteries were provided with necessities. He was all things to all people, desiring in his heart from youth to acquire the Holy Spirit itself. Cities and churches were built and renovated, and others were erected and consecrated to the glory, praise, and honor of our Lord and salvation, Jesus Christ, thereby strengthening the might of his fatherland and his Christian nation.

He founded a temple to the glory of Jesus, the Son of God, at the placed called "Ravanica." The temple was founded on four columns; and its height and beauty were astonishing. It was adorned with frescoes depicting the Son of God, His holy Mother, His saints, His innumerable wonders, and His suffering, which was done so that we could be elevated to our first honor. The temple was adorned with gold and different colors. Silver and gold-cover platters enriched the temple, as well as calyxes, plates, censers, small censers, large fans, dishes, and glasses for serving. In addition, there were miniature silver doors embellished with gold, candlesticks, large and small ornamented icons, and curtains woven from fine linen, gold, and purple. In other words, the temple was embellished and adorned with all kinds of virtuous things. Even now, it stands as an unwithered flower and is observed and seen by all visitors. Lazar also built a wall with seven towers around Ravanica to fortify it. He erected a building sufficiently high and wide called a dining building. Cells were constructed and attached to the wall like birds' nests; and in them monks could be in peace, and all others desiring salvation could stay there. Many villagers were attached to the monastery. Vineyards and various fruits trees were planted. Lazar gathered together many monks in founding the monastery and setting up a community; and it was a marvel to all those who came to it from faraway countries. Arsenij, a very virtuous and wise man, was appointed as abbot for them. But all these many virtues were not sufficient for Prince Lazar, for he had on him the grace of the Holy Spirit, which taught him to find his place among the great emperors. Later, he created another temple which was located on the foothills east of that place, near the big monastery. He built a hospital for sick monks, strangers, and cripples. Prince Lazar, Christ's servant, rejoiced at all these happenings which brought praise and glory to God; and he spent his life with a simple heart in charity and modesty.

After many years, an arrow released by God reached us because of our sins: the Mohammedans came. Every creature is equal before God. Amurat, the Turkish Tzar, moved against us with a countless multitude of Agarens which he had assembled together. Facing them, we were like a river against a sea. When they attacked and confronted our country, there was no place to go. A beast bellowing like a lion was about, seeking to swallow Christ's flock and destroy our fatherland. The Thrice-Cursed ones were wrong. Their memory was almost extinguished from the earth in a battle din as this glorious man, Prince Lazar, seeing the armies ready for battle,[4] in righteous fervor, stood fast for God and his country. Addressing his soldiers and nobility with a martyr's voice, he strengthened and encouraged them, saying, "Let us go, brothers and children; let us go to the coming battle, taking as our example our benefactor, Christ. With our death, let us do our duty, let our blood be shed, let us redeem his life with our death. Let us give our limbs, without hesitation, to be cut for the sake of our faith and our fatherland; and certainly God will take mercy on our descendants, and he will not destroy completely our nation and our country." So he raised their spirits and strengthened them with prayers. The din and roar of arms and battle was such that the earth shook underneath. There was so much bloodshed that the traces of horses' hoofs could be perceived in the blood which was spilled. There were countless dead, and the Persian (Turkish) Tzar Amurat[5] was killed there, as well as the glorious Prince Lazar. A multitude of Turks surrounded him, and he was seized and brought with many of his noblemen like sheep to slaughter. Then, on the fifteenth day of June, this holy man was beheaded along with many of his noblemen. Lazar modeled himself after Christ and became a new martyr in his last days. He then brought the big gathering of martyrs to Christ the Lord, to the sublime Jerusalem, as in the past Joshua Navin had brought God's people to the promised land. He was buried then in a church of the region not far from that place.

After a short time, his beloved son, Stefan,[6] became sovereign of the Serbian sceptre. Inspired with much zeal, he and his mother, Evgenija,[7] accepted the bishop's blessing. Having then gathered many people, bishops, priests, the abbot, and many monks, they disinterred his father's venerable body, and oh miracle, they found it intact like a sweet-smelling rose. They took it with candles and censers and placed it in his own monastery, where it is buried, healing and bestowing health on those who have faith to this day.

These are the achievements, struggles, works, and sufferings of the new great martyr Lazar; confer on us, oh God, his prayers in your kingdom. Amen.

NOTES

[1]Stefan Dušan (1331-1355) crowned on Easter Day, 1346, in Skopleje as "Emperor of the Serbs and Greeks," a title which became "Emperor and Autocrat of the Serbs and Greeks, the Bulgarians and Albanians." Stefan Dušan descended from the Nemanjić dynasty through the male line.

[2]Stefan Nemanja (1169-1196). The founder of the Nemanjić dynasty that ruled over Serbia for some 200 years. He retired to a monastery in 1196 and accepted the name Simeon.

[3]Stefan Uroš V (1355-1371). Stefan Dušan's only

son. During his reign, the Serbian empire broke up into fragments.

[4] The Battle of Kosovo (Field of Blackbirds) on June 15, 1389. The disaster left a great impression on succeeding generations and inspired some of the most famous folk epic poetry. The anniversary of Kosovo battle is celebrated each year in Serbia on Vidovdan (28 June).

[5] Murad was killed, according to Serbian legends, by a Serbian nobleman, Miloš Obilić, who was falsely charged with treason in the Serbian camp. He made his way to Murad's headquarters by pretending to be a deserter and plunged the dagger into Murad while kneeling before him.

[6] Stefan Lazarević (1389-1427), who had the title of Despot. During his reign, the Serbian state was moved northward. Beograd became the capital in 1404.

[7] Actually, not his mother, but his wife. Evgenija was the sister of Helena, daughter of the ruler of Northern Macedonia, Constantine Dragoš, a Slav, who married Emperor Manuel II palaeologus (1391-1425). Helena was the only Serbian who became the Empress of Byzantium.

The Office for St. Malutin

1.

Give me the word of wisdom, O Word of God,
for Thou hast the wealth of grace;
so that, having escaped from spiritual darkness
and having cleansed the impurity of my mind,
I, may worthyly praise Thy saint.

From your very youth,
you have shown to your nation, O most blessed Stefan,
endurance in courage,
vigor in battle,
invincibility in victories.

Harder than a diamond and stronger than a pillar,
you have manifested yourself, O blessed one,
by your firm faith and valid hope,
because of which Christ gave you two crowns,
that you may reign with Him forever.

3

As an admirer of the Heavenly Kingdom,

O blessed Stefan,
you delight in heavenly and non-wordly bliss;
and you are in the presence of the Universal Ruler
    and God.

A thrice-luminous star set ablaze in the West
which illumined with its radiant rays
the entire Serbian and Bulgarian lands
and enlightened the heart of the faithful.

You have ruled well, O holy one,
with the imperial sceptre which God entrusted to you;
you have brought forth fruits a hundredfold
and you have entered into the unfading light.

4.

You were glorified during your lifetime, O venerable one;
[being] very rich in glory and wealth,
you were even richer in generosity and righteousness,
for which the tomb with your remnants
constantly anoints our hearts with the pleasant aroma
    of healing.

My soul is covered with many sins,
I am cast down into despair by the temptations of the
    Devil
and am enslaved by an evil and stubborn habit,
yet I pray you, O blessed one,
send illumination to my heart,
so that I may hymn your radiant memory.

We are incapable of properly praising
Thy saint, O Christ,
for he has blossomed in Thy house like a phoenix;
and like the cedar of Lebanon, he has multiplied his
    people
and has built many monasteries for the monks
so that they may admire Thee in Thy saints.

5.

Rule your nation with the sceptre,
with justice and modesty, O blessed one;
you have well pleased the One
who gave to you the imperial scepter.

You have received from Him a double crown,
and you endow a profound humbleness to your cantors.

You, O holy one, were a great lover of virtues;
and you have built holy churches everywhere,
in order that God in the Holy Trinity may be hymned
in three persons and one essence,
and for that you have received ineffable joys.

With your virtues, you looked
radiant and most handsome to everyone,
O Stefan the crown-bearer;
and because of it you received many crowns in heaven
from Christ the crown-giver.

6.

You were crowned with the imperial crown
and anointed with the divine anointment
as was David in the past,
but you have multiplied these many times
through the virtues which radiantly shine in you.

Having come together,
let us, the ministrants of the saint's day,
praise with hymns
the participants of Thy joy, O Christ:
the magnificent pair, two namesakes - Stefans -
of the same names and deeds,
together with their mother, the graceful Jelena.

Thou hast anointed gloriously, O Christ,
the illustruous crown-bearer and his only brother,
together with their mother;
Thou hast honored them with imperial crowns
and Thou has made them worthy of the Heavenly Kingdom.

Kondakion

To your nation you appeared
as a most glorious branch which sprang from a healthy
    root;
you proved yourself to be a true descendant of your
    ancentors,
and, to your nation, you have been a gorgeous ornament.

Sources:

Church Slavonic Text (manuscript): *MHM*, #479.
Church Slavonic text published in: Ćorović, Vladimir. "Siluan i Danilo II," *Glas Srpske Kraljevske Akademije*, CXXXVI, drugi razred, 72. Sremski Karlovci. 1928.
Church Slavonic text and Serbo-Croatian translation published in: Trifunovic, Djordje, Dimitrije Bogdanović, et al. *Srbljak*, 4 volumes. Beograd. 1970.

STEFAN LAZAREVIĆ
c. 1370 - 1427

Stefan Lazarević ruled Raška (Serbia) after the battle of Kosovo, which took place in 1389, in which his father Prince Lazar was decapitated and the Serbs were defeated by the Turks. A well-read person and interested in the arts, Stefan offered shelter to many artists, writers, and painters, who were coming from various territories occupied by the Turks to Serbia, which, although now a vassal state of the Turks, did not at this time feel the oppression of the Turks as much as was to later be the case.

Stefan Lazarević has been credited with the authorship of several literary works of excellent quality, but his authorship has not been established beyond doubt. The least disputed is his authorship of "Slavo Ljubve" ("The Word of Love") which has been included in this anthology.

It was published several times, first by Daničić in 1859, and then several times by Novaković (1877, 1889 and 1904).

"The Word of Love"

1. Stefan, despot to the sweetest and the kindest, inseparable from my heart and desired too much, replete with wisdom, friendly to my kingdom--having said the name, Oh God, (accept) our kind kiss, together with the rich gift of our thankfulness.

2. God has created summer and spring, as the poet said, with many delights in them: for the birds, a fast and joyful flying; for the mountains, lofty peaks; for the forests, plenty of room. Wide spaces of fields and the delicate air are filled with the sound of wondrous voices and earthly gifts of sweet-smelling flowers and grasses. But who will justly convey human nature itself, its rejuvenation and its outburst of joy?

3. All this and other wondrous deeds of God, which even a penetrating mind could not discern, love surpasses; and it is no wonder, as God is named love, as Jovan Gromov said.

4. There is no place for deception in love; Cain, who did

not know love, told Abel: "Let us go into the field."

5. Intense and fast is the work of love, and it can surpass any virtue.

6. David adorned love appropriately by saying; "...Like a holy salve descending from the head of Aaron's beard, as the dew was falling on Zion hills...."[1]

7. Young men and women, you are suited to love; esteem love sincerely and irreproachably, so that you will not in some way injure your youth and maidenhood which unite our human nature to God, so that you would not offend Him. Do not grieve over God's Holy Spirit, said the apostle, with which you marked yourself openly on baptism.

8. We were together and close to one another, either with body or with soul, even when mountains and rivers separated us; In David's words: "The mountains of Gelvij, let neither rain nor dew fall upon you, because you did protect Saul and Jonathan. Oh, the innocence of David, hear, oh kings, here you are grieving for Saul, you who have been found." "I found David," God said, "the man after my heart."[2]

9. Let the winds blow hard upon rivers and make them dry, as it happened to the sea in Moses' time, and as to the vessels in the time of Jesus, and to Jordan because of the Ark of the Covenant.

10. Let us be togehter, let us look at each other, let us unite with love in our Christ, our Lord, Himself, with whom the glory is, with the Father and the Holy Spirit into eternity. Amen.

NOTES

[1] Psalm 133:2-3.
[2] Psalm 89:20. A paraphrase.

Sources:

Only one copy of this manuscript survived until 1941, when it was destroyed by fire during the air raid on Belgrade, April 6, 1941. This copy was assumed to be the author's autograph.

"The Inscription on the Kosovo Column[1]"

   Oh, man who enters the Serbian land, newcomer or inhabitant, regardless of who or what you are, when you arrive at this plain called Kosovo, you will see many bones of the dead and around them stony landscapes; and you will see me in the middle, standing upright in the shape of a cross (a monument) and in the shape of a victory sign. Do not pass by and overlook it as something worthless and without purpose, but please, come near to me, oh, my dear, and scan the words I am offering to you; and from them you will understand how and why I am standing here. For I am telling you the truth, no less than one who is alive, and I will let you know what really happened.
   Here once reigned the great ruler, the wonder of the earth, the Serbian sovereign called Lazar, the great prince, the soundest tower of devoutness who possessed the widest expanse of good sense and depth of wisdom. Of fiery mind, he was the defender of foreigners, provider of the hungry, charitable to the destitute, and understanding and compassionate with the sorrowful. What Christ wanted, he loved; and to that cause, by his own will, he sacrificed himself and all of his men under his command: brave heroes, courageous heroes, real heroes, in word and deed. They glittered like bright stars in the sky as the earth glimmers with motley flowers, dressed in gold and adorned with precious stones. There were many chosen horses whose saddles were in gold, and they had the most magnificent and graceful riders. Like a good shepherd and leader of the most noble and glorious, he wisely led his lambs, endowed with reason, to die in Christ and to accept the crown of suffering and participate in heavenly glory. So together, the multitude of warriors with the good and great master, with courageous souls and with the soundest faith, rushed at the enemy as they would into a splendid hall with a many-flavored feast. They trampled underfoot the living snake and they killed the wild beast and the great enemy, the infernal and insatiable glutton Amurar[2] and his son: the offspring of the elder and the reptile, the lion's puppy and that of Vasilisk,[3] and with them killed many others. Oh wonders, what a judgment of God! The courageous fighters were seized by criminal Agaren (Turkish) hands, and he accepted well the end of his suffering, thus becoming Christ's martyr, the great

prince Lazar. For he was cut down by none else, oh my loved ones, but by the very hand of that murderer, Amurat's son.[4] All this mentioned above happened in the year 1389, in the twelfth period of fifteen years, on the fifteeenth day of the month of June, on Tuesday at six or seven o'clock, I do not know (exactly--God only knows.

NOTES

[1] The column existed in the place where Prince Lazar Hrebeljanović was supposed to have been seized by the Turks.
[2] Murad (1359-1389). One of the most successful Turkish Sultans. The conqueror of Bulgaria, Macedonia, and Serbia, as well as parts of the Greek Empire and Anatolia.
[3] A dragon.
[4] Bayezid I (1389-1403), ordered Prince Lazar to be beheaded. Bayezid compelled Stefan Lazarević, Lazar's nephew, to sue for peace. Serbia was to be an autonomous state, under vasselage to the Ottoman Empire. A tribute of money had to be paid and a contingent of five thousand Serbian soldiers had to be provided for the disposal of the Sultan.

Sources:

The text of "The Inscription on the Kosovo Column" survived as a copy of the original manuscript from the end of the 16th century. It is now in the Patriarchate Library, number 167, having come from the library in Sremski Karlovci. It was published by Šafarik in *Geschichte der Südslawischen Literatur III*, 1865, pp. 196-197.

GRIGORIJE CAMBLAK
c. 1365 - 1419/20

Although a Bulgarian by origin, he lived and worked in Serbia as well as in Russia and indebted these two countries to himself through his literary works, which represent a heritage of their national literatures. Camblak stayed in Serbia from 1402 until 1406, when he went to Russia. During his sojourn in Serbia, he wrote a biography of Stefan of Dečani, hymns for the church service honoring Stefan of Dečani, a report on the transfer of the remnants of St. Petka (Paraskeva) to Serbia, and he also rewrote the Service to St. Petka.

Camblak has been well known and much appreciated in Russia, Serbia, and Bulgaria.

The Life of Stefan Dečanski

"The Youth of Stefan Dečanski[1]"

Milutin,[2] the fourth ruler after great Simeon, was the father of Stefan, the high column of virtue and the crowning point of Tsardom. Even before he became of age, Stefan spent much time being affable and kind to everyone. He learned the fear of God forever, and with it he avoided all evil, accomplishing many manly deeds in his early youth. He was accessible to the people who addressed him, but was sparing with words. He was merciful to the suffering, but was so disgusted with the proud that he would not even look at them. For these reasons, hearts and minds were kindled by his love. He dedicated himself completely to the service of the Almighty, and he looked up only to Him.

Why did he suffer? The devil, always hating goodness, set in motion evil, and the accessory to this deed was his father's wife. Oh, my God! How feminine guile overcome great wisdom in our ancestral paradise! Why did it not let alone her victims? Now listen!

The queen[3] came to the king; her face was sad, and her appearance unadorned and unusual. Shedding tears, she spoke with a voice choked by inner fire. To make the story short, she manipulated her husband into blinding his firstborn son who resembled Isaac in meekness and obedience. Stefan did not know what was in store for him, although he was secretly warned by many princes and noblemen to seek refuge abroad with many of his soldiers, in order to avoid the evil plot and to ascend to the full sovereignty of the Tsardom. He did not follow their advice, thinking that God's providence was better as it works to everyone's benefit. He entrusted himself to His love for mankind rather than to human advice and help. He further remained trusting in justice and goodness, surrounding himself with mercy and prayers saying, "Master and God of everyone, the only Creator of things visible and invisible, you are the witness to their hearts, you know in advance all that they are. Human thought will confess to you, and the remainder of a thought will be given to you free. See if there is injustice in my heart. See if there is a trace of lawlessness in me. '...Search our hearts and guts with justice...,'[4] oh God, and see if these things of which I am slandered are true. Judge fairly, and soften the parent's infuriated heart; and transform this rising impulse into compassion and mercy, you, the all-seeing Lord, who has calmed down the fury of Asuim[5] the Medean Tsar in Esther's time, save me from misfortune as I am not far from an unjust judgment; and restrain my father and Tsar from a shameful and contemptuous deed, since you with your courage liberate the ones who are in chains, and since your arm is immensely strong, oh Lord, about whom many songs have been sung."

Courageous Stefan confided in God only the anguish of his heart, placing in him his sole hope for salvation. He walked around in the Tsar's palace with a pious and peaceful appearance and a cheerful natural manner. He was meek, with a peculiarly truthful mien when he faced his father, but the force of providence became silent about intentions to try him with an unjust wound and to crown him with a just crown from a life-giving hand, whose works and efforts could not be truly compared with anybody's. What a story worthy of sorrow and tears this is! Feminine guile prevailed; the Tsar's sublime wisdom was overcome by feminine cunning; parental wisdom gave way to feminine weakness. Parental warmth was extinguished by feminine shamelessness. The just was caught unjustly, the innocent trapped by slanderous intrigue, the merciful was judged without mercy--and, what a transgression! He was deprived of his eyes! Lest one of those who have not heard me well misunderstand me, hearing that I was praising Stefan and that I was insulting by my words our praiseworthy and holy Milutin, let this transgression not be, since we have his father

(Stefan's father Milutin) amongst the saints as a pious defender of our orthodox faith, a faith preserved by him without blemish, to which we bow; and we kiss the sanctity which we are receiving; and we beg him to intercede on our behalf to the Lord whose confidence he has because of his many good deeds. It is the woman's agreement with the devil which we are condemning. Milutin became slightly blemished because he obeyed her. He handed over to cruel punishment his firstborn son, who illustrated, in Soloman's words, "...A wise son maketh a glad father..."[6] but he should not be condemned for that by those who understand this matter well. Did not the great Constantine,[7] the first Christian emperor, who so excelled in virtue and sublime wisdom both inward and outward, being a good and meek man, believe the lying words of his wicked wife and order his son, Pris, to be murdered?[8] Having discovered afterwards that she had been lying to him, he had her killed by just judgment.

Did you see, my dear ones, feminine wickedness? Have you heard their easy seductive cunning? Why did not such a pious and wise man like Constantine see this wicked intrigue before his son's murder? Had he known this, he would not have brought judgment on his dearest son, but he would have judged her through whom the devil spoke. He discovered it later, when there was no sense in regretting it, since he could not resurrect his son. He did not see, because the cunning words of the wicked woman covered his discerning eyes. Only after the murder was committed did he realize what he had done. Adam suffered the same way. He knew that goodness was obedience to the Creator's will and that evil was disobedience to it. He was sublimely wise, like a superb creation; God's hand honored him with an intelligible and rational spirit, and he knew goodness and evil, but he discovered a bad adviser when he seized woman for the first time; and she caused him to touch the forbidden tree. That which they had known beforehand, by birth of disobedience, they learned to commit in deed, submitting themselves to wicked advice. Those who occupy themselves with these writings know many numerous examples from holy writing; but we have to return to our story.

"Saint Nikolai Appears to the Blinded Stefan"

In such a way, Stefan suffered a pitiful loss of his eyesight in the place which is now called Sheep Field, where a temple of prayer is dedicated to Nikolai, the great archbishop of Christ. After the deed, the suffering one lay almost half dead, pierced and exhausted by sharp pain. Light sleep overcame him, and he saw before him a man of venerable appearance, adorned with saintly attire; the light of beneficence shone on his face, and on the palm of his right hand he carried two gouged eyes, saying, "Do not grieve, Stefan, for your eyes are in my palm"; and with these words he showed him what he carried. To Stefan, it seemed that he said to the man, "And who are you, my Lord, to concern yourself so much about me?" The man revealed himself! "I am," he said, "Nikolai, the Bishop of Mirlikians." Upon arising from sleep, Stefan thanked God and God's servant with a humble heart, and he felt that his pain had diminished somewhat.

"Stefan's Exile to the Monastery of Pantokrator in Constantinople and his Achievements There"

He was then exiled to constantine's town (Constantinople) as a convict, with his two children; the second one grew up from childhood there. Stefan was ordered by Adronik Paleolog,[9] the Tsar who was then ruling, to stay in the Monastery of Almighty God (Pantokrator) and not to receive any visitors to converse with except the abbot and those whom the latter permitted. Thus lived noble Stefan, enduring courageously the suffering of exile, and telling himself all the time, "Persevere Stefan"! The Lord has said, "In your patience possess ye your souls,"[10] and, in the book of sublime wisdom, it was written: "He tried them like gold in the hearth with all kinds of trials. He received them as a vain sacrifice." Stefan never stopped offering thanks, remembering the apostle's words: "...Be thankful...."[11] He often prayed, going down on his knees many times; and when the brotherhood gathered to pray, according to the rules, he was the first to stand without moving until the end of the service, so that the abbot himself, and, indeed, all the monks, admired his vigilance and zeal. Because of this, he was liked and pitied by everyone; and they showed him all kinds of attention; and often they spoke to him with great benefit to themselves, as he talked to them about the ascetic practices of holy writings. In the middle of his talk, he would quote the apostle who taught that the suffering we have in the present cannot be compared with the future glory to be revealed to us by God, and that "the more a man becomes old and decrepit outwardly, the more he is rejuvenated inwardly."[12] In such a way, he put his own suffering in second place, bearing in mind the benefit of the monks who came to him; and with his calm words, his teaching increased. He relieved the ailments of those who were fasting. These deeds were not hidden from the Emperor; and he heard also about the exemplary living of this man; and he was full of admiration for Stefan, embracing him strongly with love, and receiving him often in his palace and talking to him about many useful things. Such is virtue; it attracts those who love goodness, while the evil ones are ashamed of it.

As the fifth year of his stay there was ending, a vigil of the whole congregation was made, according to the old rules of the monastery, to the honorable and instructive memory of the miraculous Father Nikolai. Many candles were lit; and there were many offerings of incense. Stefan was standing in his assigned place, sighing from the depth of his soul[13] and praying with a grieving heart. As they were sitting down in the middle, according to the custom and the service, having read together the life and miracles of this great Saint Nikolai, Stefan, sitting on the chair because of much exertion, dozed and saw with his soul's eyes that godly man of his who came in front of him saying, "Do you remember what I told you when I appeared before?" Stefan, thinking about it, fell on the ground, recognizing that it was the great Nikolai who spoke, but being unable now to recall what had been said. The merciful one said, "I told you not to grieve, since your pupils were in my hand; and I showed them to you." Stefan showed his recollection by going down at the saint's feet and asking for forgiveness. The latter showed himself, saying, "What I told you then I am now sent to fulfill," and bestowing sight in this manner, he raised him; and making the sign of the cross on Stefan's face, Nikolai touched the corners of Stefan's eyes, saying, "Our Lord, Jesus Christ, who has given sight to a man blind since birth, is now giving sight to these eyes." Then the saint became invisible, and Stefan came to his senses, trembling--oh, unutterable mercy, oh Christ!--and he saw as well as ever. Taking a staff, he walked, and in this way he left the church and went to his cell. There he fell down to the ground, and shed tears for a long time from his newly bestowed pupils which brought tearful gifts to their receiver. He beat against his chest, and pouring earth and ashes over his body and undergoing many torments and tortures, he deemed himself unworthy of such mercy. Such are the saints; when they are honored as the greatest, their wisdom is the humblest. When he stopped crying, having covered his eyes with a kerchief, he went with his staff again to the church, and stood there as was his custom. His sublime thoughts concealed him thus from the others, and nobody realized that he had the power of his eyesight until the day when God chose him to rule with justice and appointed him as the shepherded of the fatherland, as was related above.

"Stefan Dečanski Erects the Dečani Monastery As His Legacy"

Since the holy man Stefan Dečanski held most strongly to his inexpressible desire to please God, he constantly kept thinking: "What shall I render unto the Lord for all his benefits to me?"[14] He then ordered a temple to be built to the glory of Christ Almighty and he put all of his zeal into it. He traveled around his whole region and visited many different places, looking for a suitable place for such an undertaking. He found a place in the "Hvostanski"[15] area called "Dečane," and when he had examined it well, he thanked God for His favor with copious tears; and then, turning to the noblemen who were with him, said"...How awesome is this place! This is none other but the house of God...."[16] as Jahov[17] used to say. The noblemen said, "We heard the most glorious prophet among emperors, David, when he spoke in a psalm to God about an emperor. 'Thou hast given him his heart's desire, and hast not withheld the request of his lips....'[18] Now we discover it by deeds themselves." The king told them, rejoicing, "What is more desirable for me than that my zeal agree with my distinguished God-loving friends and that they agree with this place." So was his wisdom demonstrated.

Soon he ordered stonemasons to come, and the building foremen from the coastal towns were introduced to him. He himself stayed in tents which had been set up for him; and he admired the beautiful location which lay on the highest place adorned by all kinds of trees. The place was flat and at the same time green, fertile, and full of branches. The most delicious water gushed out from big springs in all places there and a clear stream passed through it whose water gives color to the face before the taste, and afterward, good effect to the body so no one could drink enough of it. Very high mountains surrounded it from the west side, closing it off with their steep slopes dominated by healthy winds. On the eastern side, a large field adjoined it, watered by the stream mentioned above. Such was this place, worthy of the honor of the monastery being built here. He first built a wall around it sufficiently long and wide and fortified with many columns. The gate of the monastery faced the front of the church and leaning somewhat to the south. Above them he built a very high fortified column, equal to the height of the church. On the sides of the wall all around, the monks hollowed their cells like some birds' nests so that the prophet's words would be realized for them: "I was like a bird alone on the wall"[19] He built a big dining table in a separate building glorifying its maker with its splendor; a spacious kitchen and bakery were constructed, as well as the abbot's quarters, a marvelous work worthy of mention. All these were built beautifully, one after the other, and covered with plenty of lead. In the middle of it all, the magnificent Stefan erected a temple worthy of God; it was long and wide inside, and its height was such that the eyes became tired looking up. Columns sculpted from marble supported it, and it was adorned with painted vaults. From outside, it was composed of marvelous polished pieces of marble, dark red and white interspaced. With the highest skill, all the stones fitted in wonderfully to each other, as if the whole front of the temple were united marvelously into one stone. It was done with skill, and appeared in some indescribable goodness like virtue illuminating all onlookers. The glory and the goodness of the stone bestowed forever the greatest beauty to the temple, as well as fame to its maker, who had sculpted it so excellently. I do not have the time to enumerate and describe all its golden and silver dishes, nor its many priestly attires, silk textures, diamonds, and precious stones.

    Such was the size and the kind of the temple he made and dedicated to the Almighty God. Arsenij, a man who had applied himself in virtuous deeds and who had excelled himself in the rigors of fasting, was called upon by that angel-like brotherhood, to become abbot. Stefan contributed to the monastery and to the needs of the monks' many villages and dioceses in different places of his region, as it is perpetuated in Stefan's venerable charter even to this day, testifying to his love of God and to his zeal. He gave to the Lord all these things. Stefan also built a church to the eternal glory of his good patron, great Nikolai, outside, not far from the monastery. There is also another altar within the monastery to the south of the great alter dedicated to the honor and the glory of this same holy father.

"The Story of How Stefan as a Saint Defended His Legacy from the Violence of a Military Leader"

I shall present to your favor another testimony[20] even worse than the first one, since my own eyes saw it and there were many other witnesses. I am talking about Junac,[21] whose name was in accordance with his deeds. He arrived at the monastery resembling a tireless and wild steer. He had been sent by those, who were then ruling piously, in order to safeguard the monastery, as there was civil strife in the land. Unexpectedly and frequently, warriors imprisoned and slaughtered many people and caused much bloodshed.

Junac, like the lunatic in the writings, said, "The fool hath said in his heart, there is no God...."[22] He became corrupt and depraved in his management; everything in the monastery was under his control, and he directed it as he pleased. He ordered that the abbot be given only a little piece of bread and some other necessities, not when the abbot wanted it but when Junac felt like giving it. He forbade all those residing in the monastery to visit the abbot under any circumstances. When somebody came to the abbot in the customary way for some useful matter, the visitor would, when leaving, find himself in the hands of Junac's servants, who were like leviathan dogs spying on and eagerly awaiting their prey. If this visitor was a monk, he would be maltreated and threatened; if a civilian, he would be badly beaten and his legs would be placed in a hallow piece of wood which would be squeezed with force. Blessed were they, however, who were Christ's true sheep and who did not pay any attention to the threats of that beast, but rather followed their shepherd, as befitted ardent faith and burning zeal. They brought sufficient food, even more than necessary; and they would in no way stand to be separated from his love even to the least extent. So, they kept staying and waiting for help even against hope. They kept to the abbot only, thinking together and praying together with one voice to rid themselves of their misery.

Some time after this, Junac was called by a letter to serve in the cavalry. The beginning of their campaign was in this region; he went away with much pride, leaving the monks under the guard of his senior associates and leaving instructions for the abbot to be violently abused, so that he would leave the monastery because of fear. Junac swore repeatedly that if he found the abbot there upon his return, he would kill him with his own hand. As David said, "The wicked watcheth the righteous..."[23] and God did not leave him in the sinner's hands, but saw his day coming. Having arrived at the unit, Junac went to a town which they besieged. The abbot, practicing religious discipline, spent many nights in prayer; and one night, after the morning service was over, he remained in the church while only the church servant knew about it. He opened the coffin in which the martyr lay and kissed with tears his holy hands, and called on him from the depth of his soul; "Look at the misfortune of your people, oh Christ's soldier! Look at the cloud of sorrow covering us; look at the last seizure of your property; look at the monastery which you built as God's residence and which had Junac changed into a robbers' cave. See all this and do not remain quiet." Having said this, he left the church.

At that time, Junac was sleeping with his friends in the cavalry, and he dreamed that he was coming back from the cavalry and that he was passing through the monastery on his way to the church, and that as he passed by the porch and entered the so-called Tsar's door, he rushed to the table of the abbot in order to kill him with an iron stick. An awesome-looking man, adorned with sovereign's robes, met Junac there, having come out from where the coffin stood. His beard was long and streaked with white, and he looked as if he had stepped out of a painting. He hit Junac on his face and his chest with the candleholder, which he held in his hand, with such a strong blow that the candleholder broke in half. Junac turned around and ran away, but the awesome one, having overtaken him, hit him with the other half of the candleholder, as if with a spear, in the middle of his back, on his spine, and on his right arm, saying,

"This is revenge for you, so that you will learn not to persecute my monastery and my people." Having roared like the beast which he resembled and having jumped from his sleep, Junac became weak and groaned very loudly, frequently putting his hand on the places which underwent God-sent punishment. He tossed to the left and right on his bed. Friends who were with him were horrified and stood dumbfounded for a long time; and after a while, when he came to, they asked him the cause of this unexpected spell. He involuntarily told them the truth. So he suffered, at last overwhelmed with a high fever; and when he was brought to the monastery, he lay there for seven weeks while his body decayed and his bones showed through in places. Even his entrails were visible, and he decayed in such a way that the stench of his wounds nauseated all those who were present in the monastery. His tongue fell off and his teeth split from his great wickedness, and one could see him who had been proud lying like a corpse already dead and decayed long ago. A stunning spectacle for the eyes and a disconsolate matter for tears! To understand it with a subtle mind is something most horrifying. Oh, miracle, his soul did not expire first with the disintegration, which is peculiar to the body, taking place last as is nature's way; but it was the body which decayed first in a horrible and unusual way. The soul was kept within by force as a lesson to others. Finally, he had to give it up. Oh, what a good lesson, oh, what prompt intervention by Stefan, with a compassion so characteristic of him for his servants! The agitation ceased immediately, the noise subsided, and the carousing quieted down. The commotion which took place in the middle of the monastery was gone, and the company which caused it was expelled. To sum it up, having sent Stefan, the Lord cleansed his people's country. Hear, oh you who offend God, and who desire to seize church property; hear, and run away as if from fire! Let this awesome story make you wise, as, moreover, it was written: the death of your brother should be a lesson to you.

NOTES

[1] Stefan Uroš III - Dečanski (1321-1331). Dečanski stands for the famous Monastery Decani not far from the town of Peć, which Stefan Uroš founded.
[2] Milutin - Stefan Uroš II (1281-1321) occupied

Skoplje and made it the capital of the Serbian state.

[3] Camblak's mysogenia might also be due to the Queen's foreign birth. She was Greek.

[4] Jeremiah 11:20.

[5] Ahasuerus in the Book of Esther.

[6] Proverbs 10:1

[7] Constantine I The Great (324-337). The first Byzantine Emperor who became a Saint after his death.

[8] This event has not been historically confirmed.

[9] Andronicus II Palaeologus (1282-1328), The Byzantine Emperor.

[10] Luke 21:19.

[11] Colossians 3:15.

[12] II Corinthians 4:16.

[13] Stefan's manner of praying indicates "Hesychast"--practice of uninterrupted prayer involving the entire human being--soul, mind, and body.

[14] Psalm 116:12.

[15] Hvostanski, the area around Peć and Dečani in Southern part of Yugoslavia.

[16] Genesis 28:17.

[17] Jacob.

[18] Psalm 21:2.

[19] Psalm 11:1. A paraphrase.

[20] In the first testimony, similar arbitrary acts were described and committed by an official appointed by the emperor Jelena.

[21] Junac--steer.

[22] Psalm 53:1.

[23] Psalm 37:32.

Sources:

This biography exists in two different manuscript versions: a Bulgarian recension printed in the fourth volume of "The Archive for Yugoslav History" and the Serbian recension, a superior one, in the writing of Vladislav Gramatik. Safarik published and edited the Serbian recension *Glasnik Društva Srpske Slovesnosti* (The Herald of the Society of Serbian Letters), **II** (1859) pp. 35-94.

A DISCIPLE OF DANILO II
14th Century

Unfortunately, the name of this talented writer is unknown. He wrote the biography of his "master" sometime between 1337 and 1340. He also compiled the biographies written by Danilo in a *Collection* and he added the *Life of Archbishop Joanikije I*, written by some monk from the Monastery Sopoćani, as well as a biography of Stefan Uroš III of Dečani, which he himself had written. He also left some information concerning the first few years of the rule of Stefan Dušan, the mightiest medieval Serbian ruler from the Nemanjić dynasty, and the only one who did not become a saint.

The works of Danilo's disciple excel in their artistic and stylistic qualities. He had a keen sense of the dramatic and his narration is vivid and exciting. He was unable to completely avoid the stock phrases and epithets common in hagiographic medieval Serbian literature, yet the amount of realistic details in his works is usually high for the period in which he wrote. It should be also mentioned that his depiction of the attack of the Catalans on Mt. Athos monasteries is a unique descriptive record concerning this matter.

The Lives of Serbian Kings and Archbishops

"The Life of Danilo II"
[Excerpts]

At the time when my blessed master was on the Holy Mount, as we have described above, many infidels rose up, and, having gathered a strong army, invaded many territories of the Greek land, as far as Constantinople; and they devastated everything and led prisoners into captivity. The sight was uncommon and amazing. For, having started the war, they came with their armies to the Holy Mount; and after having surrounded it, they plundered all the wealth treasured there, and inflicted serious devastation; while that holy place known as Hilandar was much afflicted and in great peril because of the attacks of the infidels. And inside the walls [of the monastery], the pious and God-fearing men took refuge, among them my master, too, and a great multitude of people from the country of that monastery's nationality, who took shelter there with their wives and children.

And in that year occurred the worst evil of all evils: all mankind was perishing from hunger, but a large group of such people was fed by that glorious Monastery Hilandar for a long time. There was such a calamity that men and animals began to die of hunger. Lo, children gnawing at the breasts of their dead mothers were dying themselves; and men with mouths gaping because of hunger stumbled and fell down as if drunk and, overcome by hunger, could not even keep their eyes open. Others among them, who were lying flat and grazing on grass like animals, were dying. And many of the monks who were at that monastery, unable to endure such misery, abandoned this master of mine, the venerable abbot Danilo, and fled away. But who is the one who could escape that which had been declared by God? For the infidels, having captured those, killed some among them and led others into captivity.

Yet this blessed [man], who devoted his life to the church and who was willing to die for it, did not abandon it when he saw its great suffering. For he understood that this calamity was God's punishment, and that, therefore, all were suffering because of God's wrath. He then spent three years and three months in one and the same place in the tower of that monastery, enduring such affliction and misery that it seems to me, my beloved ones, that the wars and horrors of that period were similar to the anguish which Jerusalem suffered at the hands of Titus, the Roman emperor. For when he attacked Jerusalem, each person in that city was exposed to the blade of the sword and to other oppressions which can scarcely be described. Men gnawed at their belts and boots; and others ate even their very filth. Such horror could be seen at the time the Holy Mount suffered devastation at the hands of enemy. For those infidel nations: Franks, Turks, Tatars, Magyars, and Catalans, and other nations of various names, having set foot on the Holy Mount, at that time burned many holy churches and robbed all the wealth treasured there and led prisoners into captivity; and those few who remained were dying the cruelest death--hunger. There was no one to bury them but the beasts; and the fowls from the sky feasted on their corpses.

* * * * * *

A short while after the departure of those infidels

from the Holy Mount, it was learned that they were preparing to return again to attack the holy Monastery Hilandar and the venerable Abbot Danilo, in order to accomplish their goal. Like wild beasts, they gnashed their teeth at this master of mine, saying, "If we catch him, we shall be able to take great wealth from him." They, therefore, thought of various treacherous methods to use in order to lay their hands on this venerable [man]. When my master heard of their intention to return, he took two monks and a few soldiers with him and went to the Russian monastery of St. Panteleimon, to see his spiritual father and to pay his respects to him [for] he was aware of the infidels' intention to kill him.

When he arrived at the monastery, he paid homage to the holy church and, having taken his spiritual father with him, he ascended into the tower. There, two of them spent day and night talking about spiritual matters. Those infidels found two men from the Hilandar area who were dear to my master, their names being Nikola and Djordje, and they promised them a lot of gold if they would hand the venerable [man] over to them. Those [two], prompted by the Devil, promised to do it. And while the venerable [man] was still in the aforementioned Russian monastery, those infidels arose and started to advance toward Hilandar. Upon hearing that the venerable [man] had left, they found the two men they had won over and sent them to the tower in which the venerable [man] was, and once they [the two] were in, to let them [Catalans] in, also. These two, arriving during the night, began calling, identifying themselves by name, and asked that the gates be opened immediately, for they had come to see the venerable [man] on some urgent errand concerning Hilandar. However, the monks of this monastery [St. Panteleimon], being themselves afraid of the infidels, did not open [the gates] and did not inform the venerable [man] of their [arrival].

Then, during matins, they informed the venerable [man] of this. He ordered the two to be brought before him. And when they came, the master began to ask them, "What did you come for?" And they told him such things as would conceal their treachery. He, being truly innocent, believed every word and trusted these liars, unaware of their treachery. And at dawn, when the blessed [abbot Danilo] was walking around [inside] the tower, chanting Daily Offices, he looked at the crest of a hill and noticed something like huge birds flying toward the

monastery which he was in. After a short while, as the
light grew brighter, he saw numerous troops of infidels
advancing; they suddenly surrounded the monastery and
began their victorious attack; and making a loud noise,
they penetrated the [exterior] walls of the monastery,
jumped inside [the inner court] as if possessing wings;
and like wild beasts, they grabbed everything. Then,
they started calling those [men] they had persuaded to
betray the venerable [man], and they told the residents
of that monastery, "If you want us not to harm you, hand
over to us (they named him) the blessed [man]. If you
fail to do so, all your property shall be destroyed by
fire." And they immediately set fire to the holy church
and all the buildings of that monastery; and having
collected a great pile of wood, they placed it around
the tower in which the venerable [man] was, and having
brought tree branches and boards, straw and flax, they
set it aflame; and the tower caught fire and burned like
a fiery oven. And those evil and godless warriors fed
the flames which rose higher and higher. The soldiers
of the venerable [man] who happened to be there hit
many infidels with their arrows. Those two aforementioned liars tried to persuade those in the tower to
hand the venerable [man] over. And my master, when he
became aware of their treachery, being endowed with
cleverness from his very youth, used it on this occasion. There was a chapel on the top [floor] of that
tower and [its doors] had strong iron locks; and he,
having secretly taken the keys, told those who wanted to
betray him: "Brethren, come inside the chapel to say our
prayers and to say goodbye to one another, for I am
parting from you through the death I anticipate." In
the course of this action, the blessed [man] reached
heaven itself by his fervent prayer, beseeching the Lord
for help; to his soldiers, however, he had said that
after these two had entered the chapel, they should jump
them and seize their weapons and lock them inside the
chapel. And when they all had entered the chapel, including the venerable [man], totally unaware of what was
to happen, the soldiers of the blessed [man], having disarmed the two, rushed outside together with the venerable
[man] and locked the two inside [the chapel]. And the
fiery flame began to reach the door, but the blessed
[man], having found there some water, put it out. This
he had to do several times. After he had used up all the
water, he found a pot with a little wine in it and used

it to extinguish the flame. And God, who never abandons His people, who preserved the three youths in the fiery furnace and who transformed flames into dew, manifested similar mercy toward him [Danilo], too, for one was able to notice a wonderfully cool breeze that blew from Mount Athos which cooled the fiery heat and dispersed the clouds of smoke, for [the infidels] had attacked the venerable [man] fiercely from dawn until noon.

Then the infidels went outside the walls of the monastery, for they wanted to eat their meal. Suddenly there was a commotion and confusion among them and, grabbing their weapons, they swiftly jumped on their horses and one could see them galloping away. And my master thought that they were playing one of their tricks or that they were going to bring reinforcements, so that having brought a strong army, they would accomplish their goal. And he watched for many hours for them to return. [In the meantime] calling from the depth of his soul and shedding warm tears, he prayed to the Lord, saying, "O Lord, all my longing is known to Thee, my sighing is not hidden from Thee."[1] And one could not see the enemies return; but the blessed one heard about the misfortune which befell them: their leaders departed with the main forces and they were left alone; and, therefore, they fled to join them [the main forces], being afraid of defeat.

My gracious protector, having seen such a victory over his enemies, began to speak; and he thanked the Lord of all [creatures], by whose intercession the attack of these proud ones was thwarted. He then left the place, and having mounted his horse, departed with those soldiers granted him by God. He arrived at the monastery [dedicated] to the Forty Holy Martyrs, located on the seashore, known as Xiropotamu, which was entirely decorated and supported by the pious Father Master Sava through his generous donation of gold; and there, he [abbot Danilo] inscribed himself and his parents in the commemorative book. He spent several days there and then returned to his cell in Hilandar, praising God for everything. And those infidels and infamous pagans to whom I refer when speaking of the cruel death of sinners, having come to the Holy Mount, remained there for three years and three months, maliciously inflicting suffering. Human corpses were like the cut grass of the meadow, for there was no place where there were no dead lying. Holy churches and many houses were torn down and many settlements were destroyed, so that it is difficult even to tell where they used to be. And who could describe the cruel suffering that their rampage inflicted upon a large part of the country? For there was not a single home where there was no mourning. And when they laid all in ruin and could not find food even for themselves, they decided to go back as far as Constantinople, boasting that they were going to use their power to devastate many countries.

NOTES

[1] Psalm 38:9.

Sources:

Church Slavonic text published in: *PK*; *ŽK*.
Serbo-Croatian translation published in: *KFD*; *SSK*, III.
Život kraljeva i archiepiskopa srpskih od Archiepiskopa Danila II. Lazar Mirković, tr. Beograd: Srpska književna zadruga. 1935.

"The Life of Stefan Dečanski"

In the year this most august King Uroš the Third, inherited the throne of his father, as we have described at the beginning of this biography, he also crowned his beloved son king and gave him the title Stefan the Crown-Price[1] and promised to give him as much as half of his entire kingdom and a sizable portion of his glorious wealth and privileges. And when this took place, this Christ-loving young man served him in the fear of God, as one should, with awe and respect, being obedient to his father [and] awaiting that which had been promised to him. After many years had gone by, his beloved son, Stefan the Crown Prince, was at the age when he should receive an appropriate part of his father's state where he could reside separately with his [retinue]; his father gave him the land of Zeta.

And after he had lived there for a long time in compliance with the will of his father and in obedience to him, by the instigation of the Universal Enemy, the old Devil, who, from the very beginning, has been the enemy of everything that is good and an adversary of mankind; by whose machinations spring evil and destructive deeds--

anger, rage, calumnies, offences, murders--who is known from the beginning of the world as the apostate of the Christian faith; who elevated himself by his own will and who boasted of his intelligence, saying, "I will ascend above the heights of the clouds, I will make myself like the Most High,"[2] and who, because of such pride deserted the angels, had the light of God taken away from him, and was thrown from the heights to the earth; by his instigation, this honorable King Uroš the Third conceived hatred for his beloved son, and instead of [feeling] great love for [him], he despised him with intense hatred. And this son of his implored him and said; "Father, 'you know that I never transgressed against your commandments'[3] nor did I neglect your words; but I have served you from my youth in the fear of God, always in good faith and purity, while day and night I studied your words full of divine wisdom, trying to understand them. For I did not adhere to those who think evil, nor did I envy those who indulge in sin; 'Our heart has not turned back, nor have our steps departed from thy way.'[4] Did I ever sin against you or did I ever work behind your back? But you know everything, [you know] that I am not guilty of any such offence. What is happening to me because of your anger and displeasure is, having elevated me, you, in fact, debased me. Yet all that I beg and implore of you is to grant me that which your God-loving lips promised me: to let me live [enjoying] your love every day of my life and to behold the remarkable beauty of your God-illumined person."

However, his father paid no heed to such words, but rather his anger increased; [and] he desired to condemn his son to a cruel death at the instigation of the aforementioned Universal Enemy. And having gathered the soldiers of his mighty army, he moved against his son in the interior of Zeta, as far as the city of Skadar. And there he caused much destruction in his [son's] state: he ordered vineyards and many various fruit trees to be cut down to their roots; and he also ordered fields which were rich with grain, which provide food for the nourishment of men, to be totally destroyed; and the very palace of his son [located] below the city of Skadar, on the bank of the river Drimac, with many beautiful edifices, he ordered to be laid in ruins.

His son, the aforementioned Crown Prince Stefan, having fled across the river Bojana, stayed there with his noblemen and with a part of his army; and this father of his, the most august king, began to dispatch some of his illustrious noblemen to ask him to come to him; he kept sending him [messages], worded decietfully, with which [he intended] to lure him in order to capture him. And he [the son] guarded by God and protected by the Holy Spirit, saw through these words of his father [and knew] that they were not to his benefit; and he declined to come at that time. But having exchanged many envoys with his father until his requests and demands were accepted [and] his suspicions were dissipated, he returned to his father, [who] by dreadful oaths and many promises [invoking] the Lord God and the Mother of God [as witnesses], made peace with his son and returned to his own state.

However, still nurturing in his heart his original evil thought and having never abandoned the aforementioned hatred toward his beloved son, he was unable to restore a sincere love for his son; but, inciting himself with great cruelty in his heart, he again began to raise his anger against him, stronger than before, until everyone became aware of his malicious hatred [inspired] by conceit. And this God-loving youth, his son, having seen so much malice and hatred rising against him and the irreconcilable will of his father, could do nothing else but make known his innermost thoughts and his sorrow to the Lord, crying to Him with great heartful sadness and speaking through tears, "O Lord Jesus Christ, the Son of the Eternal Father, O Sabaoth God of Israel, the One glorified in the Trinity, together with Thy good and Life-creating Spirit, Thou art my hope and my trust; and I, boasting with Thee, exclaim 'The Lord is my helper, I shall not be afraid; what can man do to me when Thou art my power and stronghold.'[5] Look down from Thy holy dwelling place and behold my misery and the diabolical envy turned against me by my own father. For Thou knowest, O Ruler of all, O Lord, whether I am guilty before my father of any malice or deceit. Be Thou the judge and give to each of us according to our deeds. For lo, not as his beloved son, but as a foreign warrior have I been persecuted by him. Yet I know that those who fear Thy name see the fulfillment of the prophecy of the ancestor of God, David, who said 'The Lord is near to all who call upon Him, to all who call upon Him in truth. He fulfils the desire of all who fear Him; He also hears their cry, and saves them;'[6] and 'The eyes of the Lord are toward the righteous and His ears toward their cry.'"⁷ He also sent God-pleasing messages to his father, saying: "Remember, O my Master and father, that you yourself suffered many afflictions and tribulations, and that no one saved you from them but God alone, in whose hands all lies, and [who] elevated you with so much glory. And I, your beloved son, by what sorrow have I saddened your soul or by what malefaction of mine enraged you, my good guardian? In what unbecoming deed was I caught, so that I should now suffer, anticipating my slaughter without guilt? But remove your anger from this your servant, and do not despise me, your beloved son, for lo, in great despair, sorrow, and sadness my heart has left me [my confidence is waning]."

And when his father, the honorable King Uroš, did not pay heed to his words, saying to him instead these hostile words which were not easy to take: "I want you to appear soon before me, and if you do not obey me, many troubles are in store for you," this Christ-loving young man, realizing that 'his soul is sorrowful even unto death,'⁸ said to his retinue around him, "My beloved brethren and companions, you see the great hostility of the inplacable enemy which is arrayed against us. What shall we do? Let us escape from him into foreign countries in order to avoid an untimely death. For you have realized yourself that my father is preparing my slaughter for no fault of mine." And they said in reply, "We do not want to go with you where you say, into foreign countries; but if you yourself want to avoid such death as is prepared for you, strike yourself first and save yourself from contempt." And when this one refused to do that but instead made even greater efforts to persuade them to undertake the aforementioned trip with him, they acted as those Israelites who said, "Why should our graves not be in our country, but you lead us away from here."⁹ They also said, "It is better for us, even if we were to die, [to be] in the country of our ancestors, than to find ourselves as prisoners and émigrés in foreign countries. And if you do not take our advice, we shall become friends with your father and we shall go over to him, leaving you in great sorrow and shame." Owing to the fact that this God-loving young man was in great perplexity over the nature of their words, and because he had no other solution, [he and] they [all] got up and walked away hurriedly with no desire or will left in them other than to live or die; for their strength was not great, being only a small number.

His father, the honorable king, was at that time in his famous castle, Nerodimlje; and he did not expect such action at all. And they, having joined his son in the manner we described above, and having arisen from the land of Zeta, in the city if Skadar, Wednesday at dawn, halted in the midst of Prozraka mountain and took positions from which each of them would attack with his soldiers. Then, all at once, they attacked his [king's] castle; and since there was a great lament, this father of his, having mounted his horse, escaped to the town of Petrič with a few of his noblemen, leaving in the castle his wife, the honorable queen, with their children. This Christ-loving son of his took possession of all his wealth and glory as if the Lord of All, Christ, had presented it to him.

Advancing once more, he and his soldiers assaulted the town which his father had escaped to and it surrendered to him. When his father came out, this son of his prostrated himself before him, saying, "Father, may it never enter my mind [to do to you] what you intended to do to me. For even if you planned to do me evil, God has been with me and been good to me." And he [the father] became sad, then, upon perceiving that he was the subject of punishment by the rage of God; and mourning, he wept bitterly. What happened after all this? This Christ-loving son of his took council with his noblemen; and it was decreed that his father be exiled, together with his wife, to the famous town of Zvečan, to be under guard there until peace could be made between them.

After this, he dispatched messengers to all provinces of his homeland; and when the ruling nobility was informed of this, they all came and recognized his authority; and, thus, all the provinces of his homeland fell into his hands. 'For the most merciful God accomplished all that He wanted.'[10] When, after this, a short time had elapsed, this father of his, who was in the condition described above, by God's providence (one can escape from the natural bond of death, for no one, my beloved ones, knows in what day or hour his soul will be separated from the body), when no one expected it, this honorable and Christ-loving King Uroš the Third gave up his ghost to the Lord.[11] And his remnants were honorably transferred by his Christ-loving son Stefan and laid to rest in the monastery he had built[12] in the

Church of the Lord's Ascension, at the place known as Dečani. There he lies at rest, even to the present day.

NOTES

[1] Stefan-Dušan (1331-1355).
[2] Isaiah, 14:14.
[3] Luke, 15:29.
[4] Psalm 44:18.
[5] Psalm 27:1 [paraphrased and adapted].
[6] Psalm 145:18-19.
[7] Psalm 34:15.
[8] Mt., 26:28.
[9] Exodus, 16:3 [paraphrased].
[10] Psalm 115:3 [adapted].
[11] The actual truth is that king Stefan Uroš the Third, also known as Stefan Dečanski, was strangled at the time he was imprisoned. It is believed that the strangulation was either ordered, or at least consented to, by Stefan Dušan, his son. The author, Danilo's Disciple, wrote this biography at the time Stefan Dušan reigned, and, for obvious reasons, presented Stefan Dečanski in an unfavourable light, thereby justifying the acts of Stefan Dušan.
[12] The Monastery Dečani, one of the most beautiful monasteries built in the territory of Raška (Serbia).

Sources:

Church-Slavonic text published in *ŽK*.
Serbo-Croatian translation published in: *ISSK; KFD; SSK*, II.
Život kraljeva i arhiepiskopa srpskih od Archiepiskopa Danila II. Lazar Mirković, tr. Beograd: Srpska književna zadruga. 1935.

JAKOV OF SER
14th Century

He was a hierarch of the Serbian Orthodox Church in the 14th century. In 1343, King, and later Emperor, Stefan Dušan began to build the Monastery of St. Archangel near Prizren; and he appointed Jakov, a learned and highly esteemed monk, as its first abbot. Both Stefan Dušan and his wife Jelena were fond of Jakov, and they often sought his company and advice. In 1345, Stefan Dušan captured the city Ser from the Byzantine Empire; and he appointed Jakov as Metropolitan of Ser and its territory. Owing to the fact that the population of this area was Greek, the Emperor's appointment of Jakov as the Metropolitan of Ser may have been made, among other things, because of the latter's ability to speak Greek fluently. In fact, Jakov wrote some liturgical hymns in Greek, and is numbered among the Greek authors as well as Serbian.

After the death of Stefan Dušan in 1355, Jelena, Dušan's wife, became a nun, took the name Jelisaveta, and moved from Skoplje, the capital, to Ser. From there, she administered her estates; and Jakov, her friend, was her adviser.

Jakov's verses included in this anthology were written as a part of the inscription included in the Triodion which Jakov sent as his donation to the Monastery of the Theotokos in Sinai in 1359 or 1360. At present, the Triodion (in fact, a two-part Triodion, one for Lent and the other for the period between Easter and Pentecost) is kept in Monastery of St. Catherine in Sinai. The microfilm copy of that manuscript is available in the Library of Congress in Washington, D.C.

Jakov died between the years 1360 and 1365.

"A Hymn"

O Sinai, the radiance of my light,
O Sinai, insatiable is my longing for you,
O Thou who art preserved intact in the fire,[1]
Protect me from everlasting conflagration.

NOTES

[1] A reference to the Mother of God.

Sources:

Church Slavonic text published in: *ZIJK*, I, 1902, p. 42.
Ćorović, Vladimir. "Siluan i Danilo II," *Glas Srpske Kraljevske Akademije*, CXXXVI, drugi razred, 72. Sremski Karlovci. 1928.
Serbo-Croatian translation published in: Radojičić, Djordje Sp. *Staro srpsko pesništvo: Ix - XVIII veka*. Bagdala. 1966.

RAJČIN SUDIĆ
14th Century

From the inscription Rajčin Sudić left in the margin of a *Collection* written in the 14th century, we know that he was a prisoner of some feudal ruler of that period. It is possible that this ruler was Vojihna, the father of Jefimija.

The probable date of the inscription is 1360. The manuscript in which that inscription was included was burnt in 1941 when the Serbian National Library in Belgrade, where the manuscript was kept, was hit by bombs from German planes.

An Inscription

God have mercy upon the sinful Rajčin Sudić and Kijevac [who are] unworthy to look at heaven, for our souls are extremely sorrowful even unto death; the Governor kept us five months in prison, [though we were] guilty of nothing. Lord Christ knows that we place our hope in no one but God who created heaven and earth and sea and all that is therein. May that One lead us from the lowest pit, for the Holy Scriptures say, "Put not your trust in princess, in a son of man, in whom there is no help. When his breath departs, he returns to his earth; on that very day his plans perish. Blessed is the man who trusts the Lord God."[1]

Woe, woe, how sad it is in this dungeon in this stench! O sorrow, my little sorrow, there is no one to whom I can talk to about you--only to you, Mother of God of Kosenica [monastery]; lead me out of peril, for Christ knows that they falsely accused us [innocent ones]; he [the Governor] did not let us have justice, a trial, or sentence, but he imprisoned us, the innocent, myself and Kijevac, and chained [us] into a tower; may God see it and no one else.

NOTES

[1] Psalm 146:3-5 [slightly adapted].

Sources:

Church Slavonic text published in *ZIJK*, I, 1902, by
    Ljubomir Stojanović, p. 42.
Serbo-Croatian translation published in: *ISSK; KFD; SSK*,
    III.

ISAIJA
14th Century

    Isaija was a very prominent person during the reign of Stefan Dušan, during the 14th century. He was a monk with an excellent reputation and he also excelled as a diplomat. Due to his efforts, reconciliation between the Greek and Serbian Churches was achieved in 1375.
    At the end of his translation of pseudo-Dionisius, he added an inscription and used a cryptogram to write his name.

Marginal Inscription

    It is a fact that many [persons], for a long time, many years ago, in various places in our Slavic nation, attempted to translate holy books from the very wise, ingenious, and very precious Greek into our language--[persons] whose names are not only known to men, but, moreover, are inscribed by God in the Books of the Living. After them, later in time and inferior to them, in education as well as in skill of comprehension of Greek, but especially in good deeds, in the sunset of the sunny day and the end, so to speak, of the seventh millenium, at the end of my life, I, too, happened to learn a little Greek, just enough to be able to understand its value and the difficulty of translating it into our language. To begin with, it was so arranged by God Himself that the Greek language would be artistic and rich in words from its inception; it was enriched much later by various philosophers. Our Slavic language was a good creation, for everything that has been created by One who is good is very good; but because of the lack of study of the works of honorable men of art, it did not achieve the excellence of the former. Regardless of how much [Greek] I learned, I did not want to attempt that which was beyond me, that is to say, to translate from Greek into our language, for it has been said: do not seek that which is above you, and do not question that which is deeper than you, fearing the lot of those who were punished in the Old and in the New Testament, who have displayed impertinent contempt [for holiness] and who dared to touch sacred [objects]. Nevertheless, at the request of this pious man, His Grace Metropolitan of Ser, the venerable Master Theodosios, I had to undertake this translation. For, in my opinion, it was quite natural to obey without hesitation a man who was instructed by one of the angels to receive enlightenment from Dionisius. This one was indeed a man of God, if ever there was one, for his life was such that it is a pleasure to listen to his [biography]; and it is useful and salutory to imitate it. One is not only able to improve one's language by studying his [biography] but also to enrich one's own life by imitating his.

* * * * * *

Tribulations befell all Western cities and provinces, such as had never been heard or seen before. And after this brave man, Despot Uglješa, was killed, the Ishmaelites spread and flew over the country like the fowls of the air; they massacred some Christians with their swords, others they took into captivity. Those who escaped death in battle perished by hunger. For there was such hunger in all provinces as had been never before from the beginning of the world or would ever be again. O merciful Christ. Those who did not parish by hunger, by God's acquiescence were eaten up by wolves who attacked them day and night. Lo, it was a miserable sight to behold! The country was left deprived of all good things: people, animals, and fruit. For there were neither princes nor leaders left among the people to either protect them or to save them; but all were afraid of the Ishmaelites and the hearts of the most courageous men turned into the most feeble of female hearts. At that time, if I am not mistaken, the seventh generation of the Serbian dynasty met its end. And at that time, the living, indeed, envied the dead. Believe me, not only I, an ignoramus in everything, but even the most wise among the Greeks, Livanius, could not describe the tribulations which befell the Christians of the Western countries.

You who are to copy and read this book, I ask to be gracious and not to scorn the impotence of my intellect or my deficiency; for you, too, are human and liable to human [errors]; and you, too, need God's mercy and man's forgiveness. Make me, therefore, worthy of your forgiveness, [and] ask God to save you from my tribulations caused by my sins.

If you would like to know what I am called, an unworthy one among the monks, [my name] begins with an eight, two hundred one is in the middle, and at the end is a ten followed by a one.[1] At that time [when I copied the book], it was the year six thousand, eight hundred and seventy-nine, indiction nine.[2] To God, who has allowed this to begin and to whom it has been pleasing to bring to an end, honor and worship from ages to ages. Amen.

NOTES

[1] This is a cryptogram with the following meaning: *ISAIA*.
       8 = I (Cyrillic И)   10 = I (Cyrillic ї)
    200 = S   1 = A
    1 = A

[2] The year 6879, according to Byzantine computation, is the year 1371, according to the modern system.

Sources:

Church Slavonic text Published in: *PK*; *ZIJK*, III, 1908. Serbo-Croatian translation published in: *ISSK*; *KFD*; *SSK*, III.

ISAIJA'S DISCIPLE

Hilandar Slavic manuscript No. 463 contains the biography of Isaija the Monk, written by his anonymous disciple. "Panegyric to Isaija" (title supplied by the translator) is included in Isaija's biography.

No biographical data of this author is available.

Life of Isaija

"Panegyric to Isaija"[1]

Although Isaija's spirit
breathes heavenly air now,
he left his body here on earth
as great consolation and comfort
to his spiritual children.
Isaija left on earth
a newly-erected monastery[2]
to his spiritual children,
O my Christ, [whereas]
his spirit took abode
in eternal mansions.

Even though your noble and eloquent tongue
ceased to speak here on earth,
O Father,
your sweetest sermon is
your being together with supercelestial,
reason-endowed beings.
From here, a great glory
ascended to heaven, O Isaija, [the glory]
of the one who enjoyed great fame
here on earth.

You have been accepted
in heavenly mansions,
O Father,
which have been prepared by God
for those who love Him.
Do not, in your saintly prayers, forsake
us, who are poor, helpless,
afflicted by many tribulations.

NOTES

[1] Isaija is the author of "Marginal Inscription" included in this anthology.

[2] A reference to the Monastery of St. Panteleimon's on the Mount Athos.

Sources:

Church Slavonic text (manuscript): *MHM*, #463.
Serbo-Croatian translation published in: Radojičić,
    Djordje Sp. *Staro srpsko pesništvo: X - XVIII veka*. Bagdala. 1966.

PRIEST NIKOLA
14TH Century

All that is known of this author is that he copied a Meaneum (Meaneon) for the month of August and that he was commissioned to do it by a monk named Joasaf. It is also known that Nikola lived in Raška (Serbia) during the rule of Prince Lazar (+1389). It is not known why Nikola was imprisoned at the time he wrote the inscription included in this anthology.

"The Message of a Prisoner"

Forgive me, the sinful priest Nikola,
if I made some error, for I wrote this
under very adverse conditions,
in the prison in Koznik,
while hungry and thirsty
and cold and very despondent.

Sources:

Church Slavonic text published in *ZIJK*, I, 1902.
Serbo-Croatian translation published in: Radojičić,
    Djordje Sp. *Antologija stare srpske književosti: XI-VIII veka*. Beograd: Nolit. 1960.

MIHAJLO THE "SINNER"
15th Century

All that is known of this man is that he copied a *Meaneon* for January in 1389 or 1390. The manuscript was written on parchment, and there Mihajlo added his lamenting inscription.

"My Soul Suffers

My suffering and fear of the Turks are known to God alone. On account of my rheumatism I was unable to move; but having praised God, being unable to escape, I kept saying nothing but: "O Mother of God, honored in Hvosno, save me from present tribution."

Oh, how my soul does suffer because of Turkish officials, O Mother of God, protect me, Thy servant.

May God be merciful to the judge for he gave me three large cups of wine.

Sources:

Serbo-Croatian translation published in Radojičić,
    Djordje Sp. *Antologija stare srpske književnosti: XI-XVIII veka.* Beograd: Nolit. 1960.

PRIEST IVAN
15th Century

There is no biographical data for this author of the short "confessional" poem inscribed in the margins of an "Oktoechos" sometime around 1463 or 1464.

"Admission"

THIS WROTE I, THE PRESBYTER IVAN,
SATIATED AND DRUNK FROM THE EARLY DAWN.

CONSTANTINE THE PHILOSOPHER
After 1433

As with Camblak, Constantine, although Bulgarian by origin, has been considered a Serbian writer. He lived and worked in the territory or Raška (Serbia) during the 15th century. The invasion of the Balkans by the Turks caused many learned monks to leave their countries and seek refuge at the court of Stefan Lazarević in Raška. There the school of Rasava was founded, where a number of artists were involved in copying existing books, writing new ones, painting icons and frescoes, and, in general, promoting a cultural renaissance. Constantine was the head of that school and he enjoyed the respect of his colleagues as well as that of his protector, Stefan Lazarević.

Constantine translated several works into Church Slavonic of the Serbian recension. Further, he was involved in an attempt to reform the language and he discussed it in his "A Treatise on Letters." He also wrote a biography of Stefan Lazarević. At the end of that biography is a lament for Stefan written in poetic form.

The Life of Stefan Lazarević
(Excerpts)

And when Orkan died, his youngest son, whose name was Amurad, moved on and conquered many countries in the West. Finally, he assailed the honorable Prince Lazar. The latter could no longer linger and allow his own members, let alone the members of Christ, to be severed and torn apart, but he decided either to remove disgrace from all of them or to die and prove himself by martyrdom. Preoccupied with such thoughts, he got up and went against the Ishmaelites; and the battle was fought in the place called Kossovo.

Among the soldiers fighting in the front lines was a very honorable [man] who had been slandered by envious [persons] to his master and falsely accused of treason. And this one, in order to prove his loyalty as well as his bravery, took advantage of an opportune moment and walked directly toward the Supreme Commander, pretending to be a defector. He was allowed to proceed; and when he was close, he suddenly rushed and plunged a sword in to that proud and fearsome autocrat. However, he himself was killed there by them.

At the beginning, Lazar's men held the upper hand and were victorious. But the time of deliverance was over. For that reason, the son of the Tsar regained strength in that very battle and won; God allowed it in order that this great man and those who were with him might be joined together by the wreath of martyrdom. What happened after that? He died the martyr's death [and] his head was cut off; and his close friends begged fervently to be allowed to die before him in order not to witness his death.

This battle took place in the year 6897,[1] in the month of June, on the 15th day. He accepted a martyr's death; and now one can see him as if he were alive in the great Monastery Ravanica that he himself built, evidently being taken away by them [the martyrs] and becoming one of them in heaven. Yet at that time, there was no place in the entire country where one would not hear the voice of mourning, lament, and weeping beyond compare, so that the air was congested with it, as if Rachel were weeping in all those areas and would not be consoled, not only because of her murdered children but also because of the God-elected master, because he was no more and they were no more.

NOTES

[1] The year 6897 is the year 1389.

Sources:

Church Slavonic text published in: *Glasnik Srpskog Učenog Društva*, knj. XLII. Beograd. 1875.
PK.=
Serbo-Croatian translation published in: *ISS,; KFD; SSK,* III.

PRIEST VLKŠA
15th Century

It has been assumed, without any convincing evidence, that this priest, whose name appears under the text of the record of the death of Stefan Lazarević, inscribed on a monument, is also the author of that "report." Nothing else is known of this medieval clergyman.

"A Tombstone Inscription"

I, Despot Stefan, the son of the holy Prince Lazar, became, after his death, by the grace of God, the Ruler of all the Serbs and the Danubian and the Coastal Provinces. Exercising the power given to me by God, I lived as many years of my life as it was pleasing to the Merciful God, some thirty-eight years. Then the universal order of the Ruler of All and God reached me; and the angel sent to me said, "Go"; and thus my soul parted from my miserable body in the place called Glava [Head], in the year six thousand, nine hundred and thirty-five,[1] indiction 5, the 19th cycle of the sun and the 19th lunar cycle, in the month of July, on the 19th day.

The all-honorable Master, Despot Stefan, the good Master, the excellent, beloved, and sweet Lord Despot! Oh, woe to him who saw him dead at this place;

I, Djuradj Zubović, a sinful servant of God, erected this monument.

Forgive, O Lord, the priest Vlkša.

NOTES

[1] The year 6935 is the year 1427.

Sources:

Church Slavonic text published in Karadžić, Vuk Stef.
   Danica: Zabavnik za godinu 1826. Wienna. 1826.
   ZIZK, I (1902), pp. 77-78.
Serbo-Croatian text published in *ISSK*.

DIMITRIJE KANTAKUZIN
15th Century

Dimitrije Kantakuzin, though Greek by origin, was, nevertheless, a Serbian author. His father, a member of the famous Kantakuzin family, moved to Novo Brdo, an important medieval Serbian cultural and economic center. It was famous for its rich mines which attracted both domestic and foreign miners. In addition, many talented artists resided in that city.

Dimitrije was born around the year 1435. Shortly afterwards, in 1438, the last free Serbian territory, ruled by Djuradj Branković, fell into the hands of the Turks. However, even after the capture of Smederevo, the last capital of independent Serbia, Novo Brdo resisted Turkish invasion and refused to capitulate. After two years of siege, Novo Brdo was captured in 1441. The citizens of Novo Brdo still refused to admit to defeat and immediately organized an uprising which was cruelly and mercilessly suppressed by the Turks. Novo Brdo, captured and occupied, remained undefeated and continued its resistance to the Turks until 1455. That year, after a prolonged and heavy bombardment of the city, Novo Brdo fell. Sultan Amurad II himself entered the city and ordered the execution of the nobility of Novo Brdo. He also ordered the youth of the city to be enlisted in the Janissaries and the women of that city to be given to his soldiers as a reward for their bravery. Dimitrije, a youth of twenty at that time, witnessed these scenes of violence, atrocity, and death. This experience evidently left an indelible impression on him, and he became obsessed with the transitoriness of life and the power of death. Death became an ever-present thought and vision, a constant companion, a tormentor, the central theme and recurrent motif of his literary works.

Later, around 1477, Dimitrije had another traumatic experience: according to some chronicles, Sultan Mehmed executed twelve members of the Kantakuzin's family. The fact that the Kantakuzins were closely related to Irina (Jerina), the wife of the last Serbian Despot Djuradj Branković did not prevent their execution. Dimitrije somehow survived this massacre and left Novo Brdo. For a while, he lived with Mara, the daughter of Djuradj and Irina, who was the wife of Amurad II and the mother of Mehmed, the Sultan who ordered the execution of the Kantakuzins. After the death of Mara (+ 1487), Dimitrije left Raška (Serbia) and stayed near the Black Sea. There he died, but the exact year of his death is not known.

There is positive evidence showing that although Dimitrije was Greek by origin, he wrote in Serbian. This does not exclude the possibility that he could also read and write in Greek. The preserved acrostic in his "Service to St. John of Rila" indicates that it was written originally in Old Serbian.

In addition to several epistolary works. Dimitrije Kantakuzin wrote "Life of St. John of Rila," "Hymns to St. John of Rila," "Prayer to Theotokos," "Encomium to St. Demetrios," and "Description of Dacia."

Dimitrije Kantakuzin, a poet of death, is indubitably one of the most talented and most original of Serbian medieval poets.

A LETTER TO MASTER ISAIJA

"Meditation"

My whole life, infected by sins, is rooted in various iniquities, evil deeds, and impurities, for I am a failure because of my laziness and lust and lack of repentance.

Sometimes, I rejoice intemperately and feel proud because of some passing and insignificant fame, or because of some suffering I have endured, which was inflicted upon me by my enemies, but especially by finding pleasure in carnal love, which is harmful in many ways and by which one pleases the Prince of Darkness.

Sometimes I fear death; I am afraid of the future; and, thus, I incessantly dread Death.

When I think of the Judgement of God, and when I examine my conscience, I am aware of the fact that I am condemned and that by my own free will and reason I have delivered myself to the cruel but deserved torment of burning in eternal fire.

Thus, I do not know what else could await me but the dark fire which consumes all strength.

I am miserably deprived of enlightenment, for I consciously sinned, I knowingly transgressed [and] willfully submitted myself to demons; wherefore, I need a multitude of tears for expiation.

Let my remnants be immersed in the waters of my baptism, that they may be cleansed from sin as if by second baptism and repentance.

2

What am I?
Is not my body composed of the four elements, that is to say, that I am of dust alone?

The One who holds the measures of life and who governs the seasons, who shortens the length of life for one and prolongs it for another, designated my form when I was still in the womb, by combining various designs.

He reinforced my bones; He joined them to one another; He wrapped them with tendons; He covered them beautifully with flesh and dressed them in skin in order to keep the parts together; He bestowed life and breath, endowed me with speech and adorned me with reason and implanted free will within me.

For a short while in the remote past, He granted immortality to us, which--alas, I know not how to express it--we lost because of our transgressions.

3

When we consider the other facts of life, there is bewilderment and grief everywhere [and] there are no healers and no close friends.

When assailed by frequent sorrows and tribulations, when internal fire consumes your very being, you will sigh from the bottom of your heart, but you will find no one to pity you.

4

It is useless and senseless to struggle, for there is only the path of death and no other; and it will be trodden by everyone, without exception.

We are unmindful of this and we reluctantly contemplate the place where we soon shall fall, despite our dislike of it.

The sight which I shall behold there shall be sorrowful indeed.

There, after a while, I shall be able to grasp and comprehend other horrifying mysteries--affliction affecting both the soul and body.

It is indeed a remarkable sight, oh my brethren.

5

Let us not fear death any more and let us not be afraid of the malicious threats of the devil, but let us transfer to other abodes with great joy and spiritual rejoicing.

The angels of peace shall guide us from the present to [eternal] life; and we shall receive mansions according to our virtues.

Then, rejoicing eternally, we shall be with the saints, exuberant and enlightened by the eternal and divine radiance which, to the wise and sensible ones, is the Lord, the living Sun.

Those who shall be enlightened by its sweet and divine dawn shall be triply blessed indeed, because they were made worthy of being enlightened by the radiance of the Trinity.

6

Whom shall you find among us who is not afraid at the hour of death, and who is not terrified and perturbed?

Even worse shall fare, as I envision, for all those who join the Tatar princes.

There is nothing else for me to say.

Then, who shall be saved?

Few, indeed, shall escape the Prince of Darkness.

My reason fails me when I attempt to speak of these matters; I don't dare to think of them, for I am ignorant and inexperienced in these matters.

I leave this to the judgement of the industrious and wise servants of the Word, to find the solution we seek and to untangle the riddle.

7

We all became defiled with our whole soul and body; reason became intoxicated with passion, the senses became badly corrupted, and Death entered through narrow doors.

8

Lo, the burden of my sins grows in size.
Heavy is the weight of my sins, O you admirers of Christ, heavy, indeed, and countless.

It rests so heavily over my head that it bends it downward considerably.

By bending my head toward the earth, it points toward my grave and hastens to send my soul to Hades.

My fate elicits many tears and inconsolable weeping.

This is rightly so, for did I shed tears before, did I ever mourn, did I do anything good?

There is nothing else for me to say,
for it seems to me the end has arrived....

Sources:

Church Slavonic text: A XVII century manuscript in the
    Library of the Serbian Patriarchate in Belgrade.
Serbo-Croatian translation published in: Trifunović,
    Djordje. *Dimitrije Kantakuzin*. Beograd: Molit.
    1963.

A HUMBLE PRAYER AND A MODEST PRAISE
TO OUR MOST HOLY AND SOVEREIGN LADY MOTHER OF GOD.
THE WORK OF DIMITRIJE KANTAKUZIN. (In verse)

O Gracious Mother of the Ruler and God of all,
O the Birth-giver of the Creator of all,
The Life and the Light and the Grace of all,
The Abode of all desirable blessings.

Where should I begin my lament, O Virgin,
Where should I start my prayer, O Gracious One,
With what words and voice, O Pure One,
From what heart and by what tongue?

I, the miserable one, am utterly defiled and impure;
Woe to me, I am engulfed by stench and sins;
Being a sinner, I am totally rejected,
I am entirely enslaved by sin from the beginning until
     now.

Now I come to you with my confession,
Ashamed and in humility,
With tears and sighs and moanings,
And with my hope in you alone.

Against everything in Law and Grace,
I transgressed by my indulgence,
By all kinds of diabolical machinations,
By all kinds of sins, woe to me.

I sinned more than the Prodigal son,
My sins are greater than those of the Adulteress,
I am worse than the Publican and the Thief,
I am worse than Ananias and Saphir, woe to me.

As Cain killed his brother, so did I my soul,
As Essau was impure and intemperate, so am I;
I expected to be punished by fire and sulphur, as were
     the Sodomites;
All that the ancient sinners [desired] I desire.

What evils did I not commit voluntarily,
What sins did I not commit willfully,
What abominations did I not do lustfully,
What shameful deeds did I not do passionately.

What shall I say or utter, I do not know,
What can I, the most lustful one, do: I do not know;
I have no answer for the Judge;
Which of my evil deeds should I bemoan first; I don't know.

Should I bemoan my adulterous life,
Should I bemoan my evil perjuries,
Should I bemoan the injustices and rapacities that I committed,
Should I bemoan my despondency and despair?

Should I lament the multitude of my dissoluteness,
Should I lament my extensive pride,
Should I lament my vainglorious thoughts,
Should I lament my waste of time?

Weep, O my wretched soul, weep;
Weep, O my heart and my whole, being, weep;
Weep incessantly, my eyes, weep;
Weep, all the members [of my body], weep.

I alone deserted my God;
Of all the Christians, I alone lost grace,
I alone joined the Devil voluntarily,
I alone shall bitterly inherit hell.

Woe, I have voluntarily destroyed myself,
Woe, what a distressful death I anticipate,
Woe, what a cruel departing of my soul [shall be],
Woe, there is no end of suffering there where I shall be.

Consider, O my soul, what end is in store for you,
Consider the distressful bitterness and departure,
Consider the future fear and pain,
Consider it, and tremble and fear.

I wait for the coming of an unmerciful angel,
The angel I deserve by my evil life,
The angel who won't spare me but who shall torment me,
The fiery, the unmerciful angel.

I do not know whether he has been sent to take me now,
I do not know if that [fateful] time is already near,
I do not know whether he is speeding with [his] arms,
I do not know if this is that deadly night.

At that hour, there is no help from friends and
    acquaintances;
Then, there is no help from wealth;
Neither from brothers, children, and relatives,
There are no helpers and no rescuers [then].

Then, you shall sadly close your eyes,
Then, suddenly, the tongue shall cease to speak,
Then, an inner fire shall burn you vigorously,
Then, all the bodily powers shall become powerless.

Then, painful death ensues the end,
Death and agony at the same time,
Death which takes us from here to there,
Death [veiled] in darkness like a nocturnal thief.

Who would not weep over me, O beloved;
Who would not wail over me, O friends;
Who would not sigh on my account, hearing of these evils;
Who would not shed tears over me as I expect all this?

Before my death, I am already dead, indeed;
Before the Judgement, I am condemned by my conscience;
Before [being delivered to] suffering, I imagine the
    gnashing of teeth;
Before the end [has come], I know immense suffering.

I know, I fear the fire because of my sensuality;
I know, I expect the gnashing of teeth because of my
    stubbornness;
I know, I dread the worms because of my immoral deeds;
I know that the most dense darkness shall be my abode.

May hell and the abyss console me,
May the dark bottom of Hell have pity on me,
The one who shall live in it,
The one who loved darkness rather than light.

This life is transitory and time is meaningless;
It passes swiftly and is a mockery;
As it passes, without mankind being aware of it,
So this world shall also pass.

Why was it my lot to be born?
Why did I not perish as I left the womb?
Why were there [two] knees to receive me?

Why am I unenlightened and doomed to the grave?

In order to experience birth and death?
In order to perish and be delivered to rotting?
How could one not taste the life of the evil ones?
How could one depart this life without sinning?

These few [lines] I borrowed from Job.
Thus usually speak the righteous;
In this manner, they lament their life;
This is what the heirs of the Kingdom said.

If that is so with them, what shall I do, the sinful one?
If the saved feel such fear, how great is my fear?
If they are afraid to behold the mystery of death,
If that is so, where should I turn to, then?

Because of this, I do not feel like living this life;
I, the one who does not live virtuously,
The one who does not expect a relieving and peaceful
    death,
The one who does not expect peace after my death.

It is hard to take [regular] sickness here,
When the tooth or the eye,
Or the head, or a hand, or the stomach ache;
If it hurts when one of these small parts hurts,

Then how shall I, the sinful and miserable,
Endure the ultimate sickness when it comes,
The forthcoming separation of the soul and body,
The forthcoming fear of the dreadful and dark
    diabolical faces,

The forthcoming eternal torment in hell?
How shall I endure ineffable suffering,
How shall I behold the dreadful faces of devils,
How shall I pass through heavenly places of judgement?

What do I, the miserable one, think now,
What do I have that shall be faultless?
What evils have I prepared for myself
Which now so badly sadden and scare me.

What [else], but my deserting my very God,
What [else], but the condemnation of my deeds before

            angels;
What [else], but shame for my sins,
What [else], but my tearful separation from the saints.

Deprived of my sweet Lord and God,
Deprived of the community of holy men,
Deprived of the wonderful sight of the holy angels,
Deprived of the celestial treasures and Kingdom.

O what a place in which they met me,
O what an evil transformation and perdition,
O my utter misery,
O what terrible torments do I expect.

Daniel scared me with Your Fearful Judgement;
I dread the Judgement and am afraid of punishment.
The Judge is feared by the righteous and sinners;
A merciless judgement awaits those who had no mercy.

Now I entreat you who are among the saved,
Now I appeal to you who have given up the world,
Now I beg you poor and rich,
Now you who are sinners similar to me,

Shed tears over me, beloved,
Offer prayers for me, O Orthodox,
For me, relatives and friends, for me, I beg you,
For me, all of you who expect the Fearful Judgement.

Approach the Virgin with prayers,
Pour your prayers into the Sovereign Lady
Who is the trust and hope of sinners,
Who is my refuge and shelter.

There is nothing impossible for her,
There is nothing she could not do if she only would,
There is nothing [too] sinful for the Queen of Mankind,
She prefers mercy over anything else.

To whom shall I, lustful and sinful, appeal,
To whom shall I sigh from the depth of my heart,
To whom shall I raise the voice of my moaning,
To whom shall I appeal to have mercy on me?

To you, the only Refuge of sinners,
To you, the Harbor of those tossed by waves,

To you, the Speedy Consolation of the sorrowful,
To you, the Voluntary Healer of the sick.

Do not reject me, O Sovereign Lady,
Do not be disgusted by me, the disgusting one,
May not my prayer be despised by you,
Do not turn your back on me in anger.

I have no other hope but you, O the Most Pure One,
I have no other trust,
I have no contrition of heart,
I do not even have teardrops for shedding tears

By which to frustrate the Devil,
By which I hoped to escape from the place of torment,
By which I hoped to obtain mercy,
By which I hoped to enjoy blessedness.

Again I address you with fear and love,
Again I call you with a loud voice,
Again, deprived of courage, lacking hope again,
I raise my voice to you, O You, the Hope of the faithful.

If any of the lustful ones obtained mercy,
If any of the sinful ones were pitied,
If any of the impure ones were not rejected,
If even the despised and hated were saved,

Let not my prayer be in vain,
Let not my coming [to you] be rejected,
May I not be denied the hope of salvation,
May I not go away covered with shame.

Save me from tribulation and death, O Virgin,
Save me from the frightening faces and the ugly sight of
    demons,
Save me from all kinds of torments,
Save me from fire, Tartar, and Hell.

Send me an angel of peace who separates gently,
Send a gentle angel, O Sovereign Lady,
An angel who leads to another life;
To an angel of light entrust me, O Most Gracious One.

Guide my life toward goodness,
Give me repeatedly a life without shame,

A life of joy for those who hope in you,
By [such a] life lead me into the eternal life.

Make me worthy of receiving the Holy Communion
Of the precious Body and Blood.
Make me worthy and deign me [to receive it] without condemnation,
Deign me not to be burnt [by it] but enlightened.

Deliver me from all evils and tribulations, O the Most Pure;
Save me from necessities and sorrows; do not shame me;
Grant me all blessings beyond my hope;
Put to shame all those who hate me without a cause.

Lift up my despondent mind,
Rescue those who despair in sorrow,
O You, who are the only Non-Despair of the desperate,
Save by hope those who despair.

I enjoyed your ineffable graces,
I was granted ineffable mercies,
Those ineffable favours
Of her ineffable mercy and grace.

What word can express all that,
Which of them should be first uttered,
Which should, by duty, precede [others] in confession,
Which is worthy [to be used] in praise?

Which is worthy of the greatness of the Divine Glory,
Of the Altitude which surpasses everything,
Of the immeasurable Ocean of praise,
Of twofold Rejoicing of all?

She is the Ladder seen by Jacob,
She is the One along which God descended to earth,
She is the Incombustible bush of Sinai,
She is the One who received the Divine Fire in her womb.

She is the One who was [symbolized by] the fleece of Gideon,
She silently received the Word of the Father,
She was [symbolized by] the sealed scroll,
She is the one often talked about [in prophecies], the most glorious one.

Of her, the prophets prophesized in advance,
Of her, the apostles had knowledge,
Of her, the Hierarchs preached clearly,
Through her, the martyrs were crowned.

Because of her, saintly monks rejoice incessantly,
Because of her, the purity of virginity was established,
Because of her, the weak nature of woman became powerful,
Because of her, glory came to girls and mothers.

She is the living Throne of God,
For she was the Abode of the Boundless;
She delivered Adam from his guilt,
She rescued Eve from the ancient curse.

On her account, we rebels made peace,
On her account, we rejoice with angels,
On her account, we gave up kingdoms in exchange for paradise,
On her account, we expect salvation.

It is impossible to bless her adequately,
We should [therefore] bless her as best we can,
As we should bless her with never-silent voices,
The One who is the Joy of all men, and mine as well.

You are my hope, O Sovereign Lady,
You are both my trust and refuge,
You are my shelter and defender and help,
You are my protector and salvation.

Through you, I find myself in grace even now,
Through you, I share the honor of Orthodoxy,
Through you, I shall progress forward,
May I taste the food of paradise through you.

I know that she is the light of my sight impaired by darkness,
She is the joy of my heart,
She is the one who guides me toward virtues,
She is my liberator from evil and tribulations.

Bold are my approach and words,
Boldly, I, who am deprived of courage, approach you,
Your grace makes me courageous,
Boldly, I address you with joy and awe:

To you, my Sovereign Lady, I entrusted all,
To you, I attached myself completely, O Virgin,
To you, who shall take care of me,
To you, who shall not put me to shame.

You yourself take care of me, O Gracious One,
You yourself make me worthy of the honor of the saved
    ones,
You yourself pray for me to your Son,
You yourself deliver me from bitter torment.

This confession I offer to you,
This is my offering of prayerful words to you,
This is, at the same time, a modest praise,
This is as much as I am capable of, O my Joy.

Accept, O Sovereign Lady, accept,
Accept and do not reject nor be disgusted,
Accept, O You who have accepted God in your womb,
Accept, as the two lepta of the widow [were accepted].

Give me any gift you will or please,
Give me a gift worthy of your graciousness,
Give me, O Mother of my God,
Give me freedom from evil, and the sweetness of virtues.

Rejoice, that I may call to you forever,
Rejoice, O Joy of heaven and earth,
Rejoice, O Full of Joy, the Pure One,
Rejoice, for God is with you. Amen.

Sources:

Church Slavonic Text (manuscript)
    HMM #364(436) - 1643
        #495(496) - 17th
        #353(425) - 1749

KONSTANTIN MIHAILOVIĆ
1435 - 1501

There are some biographical similarities between Konstantin Mihailović and Iskander, the Russian author of the "Capture of Cargrad (Constantinople)." Konstantin, too, was a prisoner of the Turks and he participated in Turkish military operations against the Christians. Later, in 1463, Konstantin surrendered to the soldiers of Hungarian King Mathias Korvinus and he entered the service of the latter. The last years of his life Konstantin spent in Poland where he wrote his *Turkish Chronicle*, a very interesting document with a detailed description of the historical events of that period as well as various customs of the Turks and Christians. Although some of the facts presented in this book may be incorrect or subjectively assessed, the book is very valuable not only as a source of information but also as a literary achievement.

NOTES OF A JANISSARY

After King Uroš, the Serbian Kingdom became a principality, because the rulership was given to Prince Lazar, whose wife was a niece of King Uroš and whose name was Milica. Some were his friends whilst others were not, as it happens everywhere, even today, not only among laymen but among clergy as well; and wherever there is no unity, there can exist no good by any means. When Murad learned that Prince Lazar succeeded his Master in the Serbian Kingdom, he gathered armies and advanced toward the Serbian land as far as to the Field of Kosovo. Prince Lazar also gathered (armies) without delay and left for that place. He took his position on the opposite side of Smagovo along the river Laba. There on Wednesday, St. Vitus Day, a very great battle began and lasted until Friday.

The noblemen, who were Prince Lazar's friends, fought courageously and persistently on his side, and the others watched the battle without taking part in it. Owing to the treachery and dissension of these evil men, the battle was lost on Friday at noon. There, also Miloš Kobilić, a knight of Prince Lazar, assassinated Tsar Murad. Then his son Mustafa was also murdered, but the second son, Ilderim ("lightning") Bayazid ascended the throne. There, too, Prince Lazar was captured near the church dedicated to the Mother of God, known as Samodreža; and on that spot, a high column was erected, built as a marker for the spot at which Prince Lazar was captured. Together with him, Krajmir, the Duke of Toplica, and many other noblemen were killed at that spot. The traitors who had watched the battle, remained as betrayers, which later was to their disadvantage, for after some time, the Tsar, picking them one after another, ordered their execution, saying, "If you were so disloyal to your own ruler when he needed you, you would do the same to me."

There Prince Lazar was brought before Bayazid. Tsar Murad, his father, and his brother Mustafa, too, were dying on stretchers. It was then that Bayazid told Prince Lazar, "Here you see my father and brother lying on stretchers. How did you dare to resist them?" Prince Lazar was silent. Krajmir the Duke said, "Dear Prince, answer the Tsar; the head is not like the trunk of willow, it cannot grow once it has been cut." Here Prince Lazar said to the Tsar: "It is a greater wonder how your father dared to attack the Serbian Kingdom. And I am telling you, Tsar Bayazid, had I known what I know now, you would have been the third one to die on a stretcher. But God Himself willed this because of our sins. May God's will be done." Then Tsar Bayazid ordered Lazar to be decapitated; and Krajmir, having obtained the Tsar's permission, knelt down and held his mantle under Prince Lazar's head, that it may not fall on the ground. And when it fell in his mantle, he held that head close to his own and said, "I gave an oath to the Lord God that where the head of Prince Lazar shall be, there, too, shall mine lie." Then he, too, was decapitated. And both heads fell together on the ground.

At that moment, the Janissaries brought the head of Miloš Kobilić and threw it in front of the Tsar next to the other two heads, saying, "Tsar, these are the heads of your most ardent enemies." Then the Raščane, or the Serbs, who were in Bayazid's service obtained his permission to take the remnants of Prince Lazar and they carried them to a monastery by the name of Ravanica, where they buried him and made him a saint. After his victory, Tsar Bayazid stayed for a while on the Field of Kosovo and on that battlefield, he erected a monument on the spot where his father was slain: a arch was erected over four columns and it was covered by lead and it is there to this very day. After he had lain his father and brother in coffins, he sent them to Brusa, where their funeral took place.

And so ended that fateful battle because of the treachery of evil people. Tsar Uroš and Prince Lazar, two rulers who had faithfully fought in defense of the Christian faith, were both slain by infidels within a short space of time and they departed this world.

Sources:

Polish text and Serbo-Croatian translation published in
    Spomenik Srpske Akademije Nauka, CVII. Beograd.
    1959, by Djordje Živanović.
Serbo-Croatian translation published in *SSK*, III.

ANONYMOUS
15th Century

The Lament for Djuradj Branković[1]
[Excerpt]

In the year 6965,[2] in the month of December, on the 24th day, the despot expired in the city of Smederevo.

Woe, what a terrible event! Woe, what even stranger news! O my most humble and most august and in everything most superior master, holy and most powerful lion, you are so silent and do not allow me or your spouse, our most saintly mistress and empress, nor any of your much desired and dearly beloved children to hear your voice, sweet as honey. How did you accomplish this, tell me, O most God-loving and most saintly person?

"Yes," he said, "I am silent and I do not speak because my righteous Judge and Lord has so decreed, for I had been wrapped in a terrestrial and decaying body; now I am not silent in spirit, but I am as near to my Lord God as is possible; and I pray incessantly for my [people] and for my beloved ones that He may grant them victory over every enemy and adversary in these present years."

And how did you leave us, your [people]? How shall we endure this bitter and sorrowful impoverishment? How shall we endure the dark night? Who shall dress our deep wound, inflicted by your departure? How shall we survive the cold winter and tempestuous storm and these waves after we have been deprived of our most precious harbor and diamond? With what perspicocious eyes shall we behold the sun when our own sweetest sun was suddenly sadly eclipsed in our midst and sadly buried?

How shall we look up at the sky which in its dim stars foretold us ahead of time our bitter and heavy burden? O, bitter star, why did you herald this to us? Which of the swords that harvest our life did you announce; which of the sad news, unknown to us, did you declare? Had we known that this bitter omen at that time concerned us, the miserable ones, we could have implored your Creator and our Maker, the Lord God, [to spare us from] that intolerable evil which befell us.

Where can be found untrembling legs to walk upon the earth? What kind of sorrow weakened our hearts and knees because of the departure of our honorable and saintly leader? Oh earth, oh sun, oh air and other creatures of the universe, why do you tarry? Come near, start weeping with us, start lamenting with us, experience great sorrow with us and suffer the intolerable!

It is pleasing for us to say: who gave water to our head and a spring of tears to our eyes so that we may cry our bitter sorrow properly? But the rain drops and the currents of the river water would not suffice us to satisfy our need accordingly. Where is our sweetest life hiding? Where did the light of our eyes expire? Where is that strength and vigor which, from youth through old age, was feared and admired by the emperors of the world and by non-Christian rulers and princes; for did not your wars and victories surpass the victories of the ancient and great and wonderful heroes, Achilles, Samson, Alexander, and all other mighty ones? Where is your leonine voice for which the Sovereign and most powerful Lord appointed you for glory?

NOTES

[1] A ruler of Serbia from the Branković dynasty. His capital was at Smederevo on the river Danube. He succeeded Despot Stefan Lazarević in 1427 and reigned until 1456.

[2] The year of 6965 is the year 1456.

Sources:

Church Slavonic text published by Ljubomir Stojanović in
    Spomenik Srpske Akademije Nauka, III. 1890.
Srpski književni glasnik, VIII, br. 9. 1903.
PK.
Serbo-Croatian translation published in: *ISSK; KFD; SSK*,
    III.

JOVAN OF THE HOLY MOUNT
16-17th Century

Jovan was a monk of St. Paul Monastery on Mount Athos. At the time that he was copying a work of St. John Chrysostomos, around 1600, he included his report on the suffering of people in Hungary and Serbia which was inflicted by the Tartars, who at that time had invaded parts of Hungary and Serbia. He heard of these sufferings from eyewitnesses and, in addition, he himself was an eyewitness. Jovan has also written an "Afterword" in verses which was included in the manuscript he was copying.

"Suffering of a Nation"

In the year 7106,[1] there was sorrow and tribulation for nations at that time, as Christ had predicted in the Gospel. Then the Turks emerged, together with a multitude of Hagaren warriors: Tartars, I say, Persians, Caucasians, Scythians; it is impossible to enumerate all the armies that gathered at that time [and] advanced from the East against Hungary; and they captured several cities there and plundered and occupied Hungarian provinces. They then returned, retreating through the Serbian country; then the Devil, who could not tolerate peace among the Christian peoples, incited the godless and cruel Tartars. Oh, what a tribulation then befell that land: To put it briefly: they set fire to villages and towns, they devastated many churches, they stole holy icons, and they desecrated and destroyed holy places; and then, during the very cold wintertime, they made people undress and throw them on the ground, beating them, [while] others, also naked, were tied to horses' tails and dragged; some were slaughtered, others were shot. There was no place where there were no dead lying--hills, meadows, fields--all were covered with corpses. Others were taken to foreign countries and separated [from their families]. There was a mournful lament and weeping as friend was separated from friend, brother from brother, son from father, mother from son. One witnessed mournful weeping and wailing. "Woe to us," they were crying, "it would have been better for us if one tomb had received us all together, rather than to be taken to foreign lands," they lamented woefully and mourned each other. And there was total desolation of

that country. If we attempted to tell in detail all
that we heard and saw, it would take us many years to
tell it all [and] therefore, I told it briefly.

NOTES

[1] The year 7106 is the year 1598.

Sources:

Church Slavonic text published in *ZIJK*, I (1902), p. 257.
Serbo-Croatian translation published in: Radojičić,
    Djordje Sp. *Antologija stare srpske književnosti:
    XI-XVIII veka.* Beograd: Nolit. 1960.

PATRIARCH PAJSIJE
+ 1647

Patriarch Pajsije was a 17th century hierarch of the Serbian Orthodox Church and a prolific writer. With him ends the long line of Serbian biographers that began in the 13th century with St. Sava.

Pajsije is the author of the "Office for Stefan the First-Crowned [St. Simon]," "Life of Stefan the First-Crowned," "Office for Tsar Uroš," as well as a short biography ("synaxarion") of Tsar Uroš. He also wrote "Life of Tsar Stefan [Dušan] and Tsar Uroš."

Pajsije was a Metropolitan of Novo Brdo in 1612 and the Patriarch of Serbia from 1614.

The authorship of Pajsije is easily established, at least in some of his works, because he used an acrostich revealing his identity.

THE LIFE OF UROŠ
[Excerpt]

After a few days, they [Vukašin[1] and Uroš[2]] went together to hunt, as was their custom; and there [Uroš] met his end, for he, though totally innocent, was murdered. What an injustice, what a malice, what insatiability Vukašin! What hand dared to be raised and how did it not become paralyzed? How did the earth endure it and how was the sun not eclipsed? How could the air take it? By what heart, what thought, what conscience? He [Vukašin] must not have been in his right mind; he must have lost his reason; his spiritual sight was blinded as was the case with the executioner who had decapitated John the Forerunner; the present ones, too, no doubt, lost their mind. And they murdered the righteous one, the entirely innocent one, somewhere below Nerodimlje at the place called Sudimnja. And late in the evening they carried him into the monastery known as the New Church of the Dormition of the All-Holy Mother of God at the outskirts of the town of Petrić, above Nerodimlje.

* * * * *

Near that monastery, there is a river which flows downhill and there is a village called Šarnik; and there they brought the body of the young Emperor Uroš, as mentioned before; no one knew of this except for those murderers and the abbot of the monastery and the monk-sacristan. They laid him in the tomb inside the church where divine services were officiated, which was already prepared by his forefathers. They covered it with a stone slab and they held the funeral services during the night, so that no one knew of it but Vukašin and those murderers. O Vukašin, when did Satan enter you to teach you to kill, [as he once incited] Judas against his Lord and Teacher; who taught you to take the body of the righteous one inside the church? [This was done], no doubt, by God's providence. After a short while, it became known as once before [it became known] when Cain murdered Abel and the Lord asked him, "Where is your brother?"[3] Upon which, he said he did not know and the Lord said, "The blood of your brother is crying unto me."[4] Neither could this be concealed, and soon it was known.

The mother mourned her child; and when there was a gathering in the imperial palace and when many relatives had come together and there was much crying and lamenting, they asked one another, "What has happened today? Lo, a mother looks for her son, the servants look for their emperor," and they went everywhere in search of him and found nothing. Woe, what a calamity! And the Empress of the great and brave Stefan [Dušan] came to Vukašin; and, crying and lamenting, she asked, "Where is the young Emperor? What happened? Where did he go?" And Vukašin answered, "I, too, do not know what happened. Could it be, perchance, that following the example of his forefathers,[5] he went to the Holy Mount?" The mother left crying and beating her chest; and she dispatched [a search party] as far as the city of Thessaloniki and to the Holy Mount; they inquired everywhere, but had no success, and they returned. And weeping was augmented with crying and a loud lament: "Woe, what came upon the young Emperor; where did he go; what befell him?" And all was in vain.

Soon after the story of his [Uroš'] unjust murder became known, the crying and lamenting of [his] relatives and friends was intensified. And [the Empress] went to the Monastery of the Dormition of the Holy Mother of God; and she questioned the abbot and he told her everything in detail; and she, having verified his story, persuaded the abbot to open the grave for her to see. Then there was an even more bitter sorrow, mourning, and lament; and she kissed him [the remnants of Uroš] and wrapped his body in diadem and covered his face with a shroud; and she almost put an end to her own life. Oh, what a cruel and inconsolable mourning! The abbot helped her to get up and offered her spiritual consolation; and, at last, she was somehow consoled; and they offered praise to God who had acquiesced all that, as it was written in Job, "As God willed, so it happened; blessed be the name of the Lord now and ever."[6] At last, she somehow was consoled; no one knew of this for they were afraid of Vukašin.

NOTES

[1] A feudal ruler, 1366-1371.
[2] Stefan Dušan's son. He ruled Raška (Serbia) in the period 1355-1371.
[3] Gen., 4:9 [adapted].
[4] Gen., 4:10 [adapted].
[5] A reference to St. Sava's (Rastko's) escape to the Holy Mount.
[6] Job, 1:20 [adapted].

Sources:

Church Slavonic text published in: *Glasnik Srpskog Učenog Društva*, kng. V. sveska 22 Starog reda, Beograd. 1867.
PK.
Serbo-Croatian translation published in: *ISSK: KFD: SSK*, III.

"Evil Days"

A number of Slavic manuscripts preserved records of superstitious beliefs current among medieval Christians. Some of them were inherited from paganism and survived even after paganism had been eradicated. The sample included here is an example of the superstitious belief that certain days are evil.

Regulations and instructions which God ordained to be announced to the people, because each month contains two evil days, and every man should be aware of these two evil days, inasmuch as he who is born on [one of these] two days shall have no life; and who becomes sick shall not recover; and who gets married shall not rejoice; and who is drafted into the army shall not return; and who appears in court shall receive no justice; and who hires a servant shall have no benefit from him; and anything that is initiated in these two days shall be of no use or benefit and one should be aware of it:

Month of		
March[1]	4 & 22	
April	6 & 23	
May	3 & 22	
June	4 & 11	
July	3 & 22	
August	3 & 16	
September	11 & 24	
October	13 & 21	
November	9 & 26	
December	6 & 21	
January	2 & 17	
February	7 & 19	

NOTES

[1] Dates are given according to the Old Style (Julian) Calendar.

Sources: Church Slavonic Text published in *PK*.

The Song of Death

This poem, baroque in its mood and spirit, if not in style, may have been written by one of several monks. It is typical of their preoccupation with death and an awareness of the transitoriness of this life. Those who have given up the world with its riches and pleasures frequently meditated on the passing glory of men and the world; and this poem, as well as similar poems with the theme of "sic transit gloria mundi," must have been rather popular among the monks.

The author if this poem is unknown. It may have been translated from Greek or written originally in Slavic. In one of the two versions of this poem, preserved in two different manuscripts, the title is given as "Nadgrobnoe zvanie vlastelina nekoego Grka v Soluně" ("Funeral Dirge of a Greek Nobleman from Thessalonike").

Although it has not been formally subdivided in stanzas and verses in the manuscript, it is evidently a poem. Metric pattern is maintained throughout the poem and the rhyme is used rather consistently.

Today I give up my ghost
and cover myself with dust.
I put on the shroud
and I ride on a wooden horse.[1]
They built a house without windows for me[2]
"Go and take abode in it," they told me.
Rejoice in the birth,
lament the departure,
mourn, O Birthgiver,
rejoice, O gainer![3]
My mother begets me,
the earth swallows me.

I came to you with sighing,
breathless I left you,
(I am departing, my friends,
never again will I come back to you).
I expected to reach old age
and to share joys with you,
but Death shows no mercy,
nor does it wait for ripe age,
It does not accept bribes;
no one's sins does it remove,
for it does not spare emperors because of their empire

nor rich because of their wealth;
for it aflicts mother with sorrow
and it injures the hearts of infants;
for it does not show favour to the poor,
it exercises its power over everyone.

Out of dust God created Adam,[4]
but Death parted him from his soul;
two brothers[5] came to existence,
but it did not spare them either, it separated them.
Seth was born in accordance with the promise,[6]
but it appointed his [last] hour.
Enosh[7] was building a city;
Death grabbed him to itself.

Methuselah[8] wrote hymns;
Death sent him to the grave.
Noah divided the entire world into three parts;[9]
Death plucked his soul.
Shem [covered] his father's nakedness,[10]
but Death covered him with dust.
Abraham was hospitable,[11]
yet Death was not shy with him.
Jacob wrestled with an angel,[12]
but Death overcame him.
Joseph inherited the empire of Egypt,[13]
but Death robbed him of life.
Moses was able to see God;[14]
Death was not shy with him.
Aaron was in the service of God;[15]
[nevertheless], it hunted him zealously.
Joshua issued orders to the sun,[16]
but Death returned him to earth.
The sons of Israel tasted the bread of heaven,[17]
in the desert they died.
Hannah acquired Samuel through prayer,[18]
but Death took him away for itself.
David composed the psalms,[19]
but Death parted him from his soul.

Solomon outwitted everyone;[20]
Death pierced him with the lance.
Elisha received twofold grace,[21]
but Death deprived him of these gifts.
Isaiah prophesized;[22]
Death was approaching him.

Ezekiel put together the dried bones,[23]
but it [Death] appointed his [last] hour.
Jonah found his way out of the whale's belly,[24]
yet Death made him descend into the bowels of the earth.
Gideon put God to the test with the fleece,[25]
but Death settled him into the waterless abode.
God inflicted tribulations upon Manasseh,[26]
but Death relieved him from them.
Jeremiah was protected by a stone[27]
until the arrival of Death.
Abimeleh rose from sleep,[28]
but to it [Death], he surrendered.
Daniel shut the lions' jaws,[29]
but Death vaulted him over with dust.
The three youths were not consumed by fire,[30]
but it [Death] scorched them.
John did not eat bread,[31]
but Death devoured him.
Christ enlightened people;
it [Death] tortured Him on the cross.
Christ resurrected the dead;
it took Him down to the grave.
Peter denied Christ,[32]
but to it [Death], he adhered.
Paul was let down in a basket;[33]
but to it [Death], he was lifted up.
This is the counsel of the elected ones:
If so many men and of such qualities,
who performed so many miracles,
suffered death in such manner,
and Death was not why with those
who were the elect of God,
even more so will [it] be with us,
the transgressors of the commandments of God.
For it came to me today
and touched all my joints,
it severed my tendons,
it cut me to pieces,
it disjoined my joints,
it joined me to itself.
When it saw me dead,
when it experienced joy.
Angels descended,
they gathered a crowd of people,
of all of them selected me,
they took me away with them,

and brought me before the Lord.
"Who are you?
Answer me," He said.
For the Judge was seated
and He appeared awesome,
[yet] He was wonderful in His goodness,
and brighter than the sun.
The devils gathered, too,
and brought many accusations.
The Judge judged righteously,
until my trial was over.
They led me away from there
and to whom did they bring me?
They handed me to the black Moor;
he was glad to see me.
He took me in his hands,
he gnawed me rather than bread,
he divested me of my beauty,
he conjoined me with darness,
he surveyed me with his eyes,
tormented me for a while
[and] locked me up in Hell.
There sat some [creatures]
who resembled swine.

NOTES

[1] A metaphor for *coffin*.
[2] A metaphor for *grave*.
[3] Death.
[4] See Gen., 2:7.
[5] Cain and Abel. See Gen., 4:1-2.
[6] See Gen. 4:25.
[7] A son of Seth. See Gen., 5:6.
[8] A son of Enoch. See Gen., 5:21-22; 25-27.
[9] See Gen., 9:19.
[10] See Gen., 9:23.
[11] See Gen., 18:1-8.
[12] See Gen., 32:24-26.
[13] See Gen., 41:41.
[14] See Exodus, 19:3, 9, 20.
[15] See Exodus, 28:1.
[16] See Joshua, 10:12-14.
[17] See Exodus, 16:14-36.
[18] See I Sam., 1:10-28.
[19] One of the kings of Israel and the author of

many Psalms included in the Book of Psalms in the Old Testament.

[20] Solomon, the son of David and Bathsheba (II Sam., 12:24), enjoyed the reputation of a very wise man.

[21] A disciple of Elijah (I Kings, 19:19-21; II Kings, 2:1-16). He had the gift of prophecy and wonder-working.

[22] See the Book of Isaiah.

[23] See Ezekiel, 37:1-8.

[24] See Jonah, 1:1-17; 2:1-10.

[25] See Judges, 6:36-40.

[26] See II Chronicles, 33:1-20.

[27] See Jeremiah, 13:4-5.

[28] See Gen., 20:3.

[29] See Daniel, 6:16-22.

[30] Hananiah (Shadrach), Mischael (Meshach) and Azariah (Abednago). See Daniel, 3:8-30.

[31] See Lk., 7:33.

[32] See Mt., 26:69-75.

[33] See Acts, 9:25 and II Cor., 11:33.

Sources: Church Slavonic Text published in *PK*.

MIHAJLO OF SMEDEREVO
+ 1711

After the death of Stefan Lazarević, his heir, Djuradj Branković, transferred the capital of Serbia to Smederevo, a town on the Danube, near Belgrade. At that time, the Bishop of Smederevo held the title of Metropolitan, and Mihajlo occupied that position. He was officially the Metropolitan of Smederevo and, later, of Žiča, Belgrade and Požarevac. In 1682, Mihajlo inscribed on the pages of a manuscript his elegiac and somewhat didactic poem which, similar to the "Poem of Death," deals with the transitoriness of life and fragility of man.

"Woe, Woe!

Today he is healthy,
tomorrow he is sick;
today he rejoices,
tomorrow he mourns.
Today he is young,
tomorrow he is old.
Today he enjoys glory,
tomorrow he is without honor.
Today he is hungry and thirsty,
tomorrow he overeats and drinks too much.
Woe, woe, great will be my punishment.

Sources:

    Church Slavonic text published in *ZIJK*, I (1902), p. 429.
    Serbo-Croatian translation published in Radojičić, Djordje Sp. *Antologija stare, srpske književnosti: XI- XVIII veka*. Beograd: Nolit. 1960.

BIBLIOGRAPHY

Bašic Milivoje. *Iz stare srpske književnosti*. Beograd. 1922.
Bogdanović Dimitrije, et al. *Srbljak*. 4 volumes. Beograd. 1972.
Ćorović Vladimir. *Spisi Sv. Save*. Beograd. 1928.
Daničić Djura. *Životi Kraljeva i Arxiepiskopa Srpskix*, 1866.
Murko Matija. *Geschichte der Alteren Sudslawischen Literatur*. Munchen. 1971. (Reprint.)
Novokavić Stojan. *Primeri Književnosti i jezika staroga i srpsko slovenskoga*. Beograd. 1904.
Pavlović Dragolijub. *Iz naše starije književnosti: Studije i članci*. Sarajevo. 1964.
_____. *Stara srpska književnost*. 2 volumes. Beograd-Novi Sad. 1970.
Pavlović Dragoljub i Radmila Marinković. *Iz naše književnosti feudalnog doba*. Sarajevo. 1959.
Pavlović Milivoj. *Primeri istoriskog razvitka srpskohrvatskog jezika*. Beograd. 1956.
Radojičić Djordje. *Antologija stare srpske književnosti XI-XVIII veka*. Beograd. 1960.
Književna zbivanja i stvaranja kod Srba u srednjem veku i u tursko doba. Novi Sad. 1967.
Razvojni luk stare srpske književnosti. Novi Sad. 1962.
Staro srpsko pesništvo (X-XVIII veka). Kruševac. 1966.
Tvorci i dela stare srpske književnosti. Titograd. 1963.
Schaffarik Pavle. *Pametky Drevnilo Pisemnictry Jihokovanuv*. Prague. 1851.
_____. *Serbische Lesekörner*. Pesth. 1833.
Stanojevich M. *Early Yugoslav Literature: 1000-1800*. New York. 1922.
Stanojevich, St. D-R, D. Glumac. *Sv. Pismo U Našim Starim spomenicima, Posebno izdanje*, Book 39. Srpska Kraljevska Akademiia, Beograd. 1932.
Trifunović Djordje. *Dimitrije Kantakuzen*. Beograd.

THE LIST OF CONTRIBUTIONS

A. Contributions by Mateja Matejić

1. "Medieval Serbian Literature"
2. Biographical sketches on Presbyter from Dioclea; Stefan Nemanja; Saint Sava; Stefan Nemanjić the First-Crowned; Domentijan; Atanasije; Siluan; Teodosije; Teodor; Nikodim of Hilandar; Jefimija; Danilo II; Milica Hrebeljanović [Jevgenija]; Danilo III; Stefan Lazarević; Grigorije Camblak; Danilo's Disciple; Jakov of Ser; Rajčin Sudić; Isaija; Isaija's Disciple; Priest Nikola; Mihajlo the "Sinner"; Priest Ivan; Constantine the Philosopher; Priest Vlkša; Dimitrije Kantakuzin; Konstantin Mihailović; Jovan of the Holy Mount; Pajsije; Mihajlo of Smederevo
3. Presbyter from Dioclea: THE KINGDOM OF SLAVS
   [Legend of Prince Vladislav]
4. Stefan Nemanjić the First Crowned: THE LIFE OF ST. SIMEON: [Praise to St. Simeon]
5. Domentijan. The LIFE OF SAINT SAVA
   [Rastko's Birth; Rastko's Departure for the Holy Mount; the Search Party Finds Rastko on the Holy Mount; Rastko Becomes Monk]
   LIFE OF ST. SIMEON:
   [Rastko's Departure for the Holy Mount Athos; Stefan the First-Crowned's Letter to St. Sava]
6. Atanasije: Eulogy to St. Sava
7. Siluan: Hymn to Saint Sava
8. Teodosije: The OFFICE FOR ST. SIMEON
   CANNON TO ST. SIMEON
   The LIFE OF ST. PETAR OF KORIS
9. Teodor: A Scribe's Inscription
10. Nikodim of Hilandar: A Visit to Constantinople
11. Danilo II: THE LIVES OF SERBIAN KINGS AND ARCHbishops:
    [The Life of Milutin;
    The Lament Over Dragutin]
12. Milica Hrebeljanović (Jevgenija)
    Mother's Prayer;
    Who Is This One/
13. Danilo III. The OFFICE FOR PRINCE MARTYR LAZAR:
    [Canon to Prince Martyr Lazar;
    Hymn to Prince Martyr Lazar;
    Milica's Lament]

The OFFICE FOR ST. MILUTIN
14. Danilo's Disciple, The LIVES OF SERBIAN KINGS AND
    ARCHBISHOPS
    [Life of Danilo II; Life of Stefan Dečanski]
15. Jakov of Ser: A Hymn
16. Rajčin Sudić: An Inscription
17. Isaija; Marginal Inscription
18. Isaija's Disciple, The LIFE OF ISAIJA
    [Panegyric to Isaija]
19. Priest Nikola: The Message of a Prisoner
20. Mihajlo the Sinner: My Souls Suffers
21. Priest Ivan: Admission
22. Constantine the Philosopher,
    The LIFE OF STEFAN LAZAREVIĆ
23. Priest Vlkša, A Tombstone Inscription
24. Dimitrije Kantakuzin, A LETTER TO MASTER ISAIJA
    (Meditation]
    A HUMBLE PRAYER
25. Konstantin Mihailović, NOTES OF A JANISSARY
26. Anonymous: Lament Over Djuradj Branković
27. Jovan of the Holy Mount: Suffering of a Nation
28. Pajsije, LIFE OF UROS
29. Anonymous: Evil Days
30. Anonymous: The Song of Death
31. Mihajlo of Smederevo: Woe, Woe!

B. Contributions by Dragan Milivojevic

1. "On the Language of Medieval Serbian Literature"
2. Stefan Nemanja: THE HILANDAR CHARTER
3. St. Sava [Rastko Nemanjić], THE LIFE OF SAINT SIMEON
   [Nemanja's Abdication, His Advice to the Nobility
   and His Parting with Them; Nemanja Abdicating,
   Advises His Sons; Nemanja Sees Death Approaching,
   Parts with His Son; Nemanja's Last Hours]
4. Domentijan, THE LIFE OF ST. SIMEON
   [Saint Sava Became an Archbishop and Secured
   the Serbian Independent Church]
5. Teodosije, the LIFE OF SAINT SAVA
   [Saint Sava Having Become an Archimandrite,
   Returned to Serbia with Nemanja's Remains]
6. Jefimija, The Lament Over the Dead Son Overcome by
   Her Motherly Ways;
   The Encomium to Prince Lazar;
   Prayer to Lord Jesus Christ
7. Danilo II, THE LIVES OF SERBIAN KINGS AND ARCHBISHOPS

[Queen Jelena's Death]
8. Danilo III, A Narration About Prince Lazar
9. Stefan Lazarevic, THE WORD OF LOVE
   THE INSCRIPTION ON THE KOSOVO COLUMN
10. Grigorije Camblak, THE LIFE OF STEFAN DEČANSKI
    [The Youth of Stefan Dečanski; Saint Nikolai
    Appears to the Blinded Stefan; Stefan's Exile to
    the Monastery Pantokrator in Constantinople and
    His Achievements There; Stefan Dečanski Erects
    Dečani as His Legacy; The Story How Stefan as a
    Saint Defended His Legacy from the Violence of a
    Military Leader]

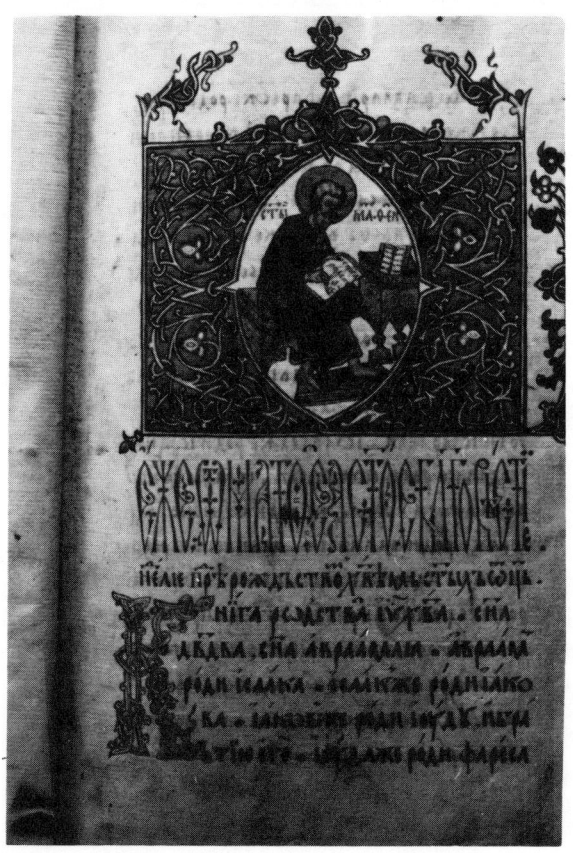

Hilandar Codex 44: a tetra Gospel from the 17th century. Matthew I.

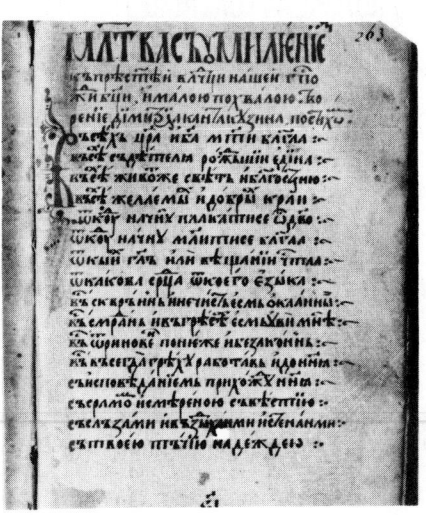

Dimitrije Kantakuzin: "Prayer to Theotokos."
(See page 175.) Hilandar manuscript 353 from 1749.

Prayer book. Hilandar manuscript 314, 13th century.

BOOKS FROM SLAVICA PUBLISHERS

American Contributions to the Eighth International Congress of Slavists, Zagreb and Ljubljana, Sept. 3-9, 1978. Vol. 1: Linguistics and Poetics, edited by Henrik Birnbaum, 818 p., 1978; *Vol. 2: Literature*, edited by Victor Terras.

Henrik Birnbaum: *Common Slavic Progress and Problems in Its Reconstruction*, xi + 436 pp., 1975.

Malcolm H. Brown, ed.: *Papers of the Yugoslav-American Seminar on Music*, 208 p., 1970.

Catherine V. Chvany: *On the Syntax of Be-Sentences in Russian*, viii + 311 p., 1975.

Frederick Columbus: *Introductory Workbook in Historical Phonology*, 39 p., 1974.

Dina B. Crockett: *Agreement in Contemporary Standard Russian*, iv + 456 p., 1976.

Paul Debreczeny and Thomas Eekman, eds.: *Chekhov's Art of Writing A Collection of Critical Essays*, 199 p., 1977.

Ralph Carter Elwood, ed.: *Reconsiderations on the Russian Revolution*, x + 278 p., 1976. (Papers from the Banff '74 Conference)

Folia Slavica, a journal of Slavic and East European linguistics, first issue March 1977, three numbers per volume, approximately one volume per year.

Richard Freeborn, R. R. Milner-Gulland, and Charles A. Ward, eds.: *Russian and Slavic Literature*, xii + 466 p., 1976. (Papers from the Banff '74 Conference)

Victor A. Friedman: *The Grammatical Categories of the Macedonian Indicative*, 210 p., 1977.

Charles E. Gribble, ed.: *Medieval Slavic Texts, Vol. 1, Old and Middle Russian Texts*, 320 p., 1973.

Charles E. Gribble: *Russian Root List with a Sketch of Russian Word Formation*, 56 p., 1973.

Charles E. Gribble: *Slovarik russkogo jazyka 18-go veka/A*

BOOKS FROM SLAVICA PUBLISHERS

Short Dictionary of 18th-Century Russian, 103 p.

Charles E. Gribble, ed.: *Studies Presented To Professor Roman Jakobson by His Students*, 333 p., 1968.

Raina Katzarova-Kukudova & Kiril Djenev: *Bulgarian Folk Dances*, 174 p., numerous illustrations, 2nd printing 1976 (1st printing, Sofia 1958).

Demetrius J. Koubourlis, ed.: *Topics in Slavic Phonology*, viii + 270 p., 1974.

Michael K. Launer: *Elementary Russian Syntax*, xi + 140 p., 1974.

Maurice I. Levin: *Russian Declension and Conjugation: a structural sketch with exercises*, x + 160 p., 1978.

Alexander Lipson: *A Russian Course.*

Thomas F. Magner, ed.: *Slavic Linguistics and Language Teaching*, x + 309 p., 1976. (Papers from the Banff '74 Conference)

Vasa D. Mihailovich and Mateja Matejic: *Yugoslav Literature in English A Bibliography of Translations and Criticism (1821-1975)*, ix + 328 p., 1976.

Kenneth E. Naylor, ed.: *Balkanistica: Occasional Papers in Southeast European Studies*, I (1974), 189 p., 1975; II (1975), 153 p., 1976; III (1976), 154 p., 1978.

Felix J. Oinas, ed.: *Folklore Nationalism & Politics*, 190 p., 1977.

Hongor Oulanoff: *The Prose Fiction of Veniamin A. Kaverin*, v + 203 p., 1976.

Jan L. Perkowski, ed.: *Vampires of the Slavs* (a collection of readings), 294 p., 1976.

Lester A. Rice: *Hungarian Morphological Irregularities*, 80 p., 1970.

Midhat Ridjanovic: *A Synchronic Study of Verbal Aspect in English and Serbo-Croatian*, ix + 147 p., 1976.

BOOKS FROM SLAVICA PUBLISHERS

David F. Robinson: *Lithuanian Reverse Dictionary*, ix + 209 p., 1976.

Don K. Rowney and G. Edward Orchards, eds.: *Russian and Slavic History*, viii + 311 p., 1977. (Papers from the Banff '74 Conference)

Ernest A. Scatton: *Bulgarian Phonology*, xii + 224 p., 1976.

William R. Schmalstieg: *Introduction to Old Church Slavic*, 290 p., 1976.

Michael Shapiro: *Aspects of Russian Morphology, A Semiotic Investigation*, 62 p., 1969.

Charles E. Townsend: *The Memoirs of Princess Natal'ja Borisovna Dolgorukaja*, viii + 146 p. 1977.

Charles E. Townsend: *Russian Word-Formation, corrected reprint*, xviii + 272 p., 1975.

D. N. Ushakov, ed.: *Tolkovyj slovar' russkogo jazyka*, original edition in 4 volumes, Moscow, 1934-1940; reprint (slightly reduced in page size, corrections indicated throughout, 4 volumes bound in 3), 1974.

Susan Wobst: *Russian Readings & Grammar Terminology*, 88 p., 1978.

Dean S. Worth: *A Bibliography of Russian Word-Formation*, xliv + 317 p., 1977.